Cool Time
and the
Two-Pound Bucket

Time Management for the 24-Hour Person

Steve Prentice

Stoddart

Published in 2002 by
Stoddart Publishing Co. Limited
895 Don Mills Road, 400-2 Park Centre, Toronto, Canada M3C 1W3
PMB 128, 4500 Witmer Estates, Niagara Falls, New York 14305-1386

www.stoddartpub.com

To order Stoddart books please contact General Distribution Services
In Canada Tel. (416) 213-1919   Fax (416) 213-1917
Email cservice@genpub.com
In the United States Toll-free tel. 1-800-805-1083 Toll-free fax 1-800-481-6207
Email gdsinc@genpub.com

10 9 8 7 6 5 4 3 2 1

National Library of Canada Cataloguing in Publication Data
Steven Prentice
Cool Time and the Two-Pound Bucket: Time Management for the 24-Hour
Person
1. Time Management. I. Title.
ISBN 0-7737-6254-X

U.S. Cataloging-in-Publication Data
Available from the Library of Congress

Cover design: Bill Douglas at The Bang
Text design: Tannice Goddard

THE CANADA COUNCIL | LE CONSEIL DES ARTS
FOR THE ARTS | DU CANADA
SINCE 1957 | DEPUIS 1957

*We acknowledge for their financial support of our
publishing program the Canada Council, the Ontario Arts
Council, and the Government of Canada through the
Book Publishing Industry Development Program (BPIDP).*

Printed and bound in Canada

Contents

Introduction: Dogs and Cats and Pointing Fingers

When you point your finger at the horizon, a human will look in the direction you are pointing. A dog or a cat will just look at the end of your finger to see what is there. Time management is like that. Though the benefits of this life-changing concept are all too easy to point out, most people end up focusing on the techniques themselves — the pointing finger, as it were — allowing themselves no opportunity to develop and refine the "vision" that supports time management in its truest sense.

At its core, a time management plan needs awareness, technique, and commitment. To succeed, you must be able to look past the concepts and see yourself on your own goal horizon. You must picture your future successes and achievements, and use them as currency for the efforts you are about to undertake. You must then share this vision with your employer, your colleagues, and your family. Without this preparation, all the time management tips and tricks in the world will simply sit there on the end of your finger.

Time management starts with awareness: awareness of the importance of each of your tasks and activities; awareness of your personal strengths and limitations, and those of the people around you; awareness of the fixed duration of a 24-hour day; and awareness of what you are doing at any moment and why you are doing it. Awareness defines the landscape of your efforts and plans. It is the foundation.

Time management also requires technique and structure. (I do not use the word "discipline" here, as that term carries too many negative connotations. Discipline represents actions or rules imposed on your life that may run counter to your natural inclinations.) We all differ in the way we work, the way we think, our priorities at work and at home, our ability to get up in the morning, our levels of concentration and organization, and our ability to accept new ideas. Therefore, it is up to you to develop a technique that fits in well with your life and will generate positive change with minimal disruption. Many diets, fitness programs, and management philosophies fail not because they're unsound, but because they are too generalized and do not offer themselves well to tailoring.

I offer the suggestions in this book as separate and individual concepts to give you the opportunity to accept and act upon those that make the most sense to you. After all, only you can implement these changes in your life, with its unique priorities, rhythms, and constraints.

After choosing your "structure" (a workable collection of time management techniques), you will then need to commit to their implementation. Old habits, as the saying goes, die hard. This applies not only to your own tendencies, but also to those of the people around you, and to the constraints of your work environment itself. Certain time management techniques may take days or weeks before they are successfully integrated into your life, and some may fail on the first attempt. But the secret to success in any life-modifying endeavor is to stick with it, keeping your eyes on the goal, envisioning the success that sits on the horizon, and knowing both how and why you will attain it.

Time management is also about change, and change is a difficult thing. People differ in the degree to which they embrace change. Some take it on willingly; others resist. Almost everyone dislikes change being forced upon them, but many are willing to undertake it if they can participate in its development and can visualize its ultimate benefits.

I created this book for people who truly want to get a better handle on their day's affairs and implement positive change.

Cool Time and the Two-Pound Bucket gives you the building blocks of a personal time management strategy from two directions.

On the one hand, it focuses on you, the individual. Not just the 9-to-5 you, but the 24-hour you. It recognizes that time management is a principle that applies to each person differently, and just as we all have different factors influencing our days, we also differ in our definitions of what successful time management means. One person's goals may be defined in terms of steady promotions and increased salary, whereas another's may be simply the ability to get home at a reasonable hour to enjoy more time with the family. Both are right; both are good. Both are attainable, without being mutually exclusive. The secret lies in knowing what is important to you, stating to yourself why these things are important, and then setting up a plan to achieve them.

On the other hand, none of us operates in a vacuum, so we will also focus on your role as a team member. We interact with others all the time, at work, at home, on the highway, at the supermarket. As such, it is important to shed light on how time management can be incorporated into our multidimensional world, with its myriad personalities, priorities, and relationships.

Perhaps most important of all, this book throws away the rose-colored glasses. It is very easy to suggest techniques for reducing workload or stress at the office. But if your boss, supervisor, colleagues, or clients don't subscribe to these great new ideas, they can become sources of conflict or worse. To succeed you will need to communicate your time management intentions clearly to them and help them learn their own techniques. They will need to understand the benefits of time management and why you are undertaking such seemingly unusual habits. This I call "Emotional Bedrock," a degree of self-confidence and self-assurance that will help you to recognize that implementing time management is a positive, healthy, and responsible thing to do.

Wherever possible, I've included the "Yes, but . . ." counter-argument. If, while reading any of the principles and techniques in this book, you find yourself thinking, "Yes, but that's not going to work here because . . ." look for the "Yes, but . . ." icon to see whether your particular objection has been addressed. If it hasn't, or if you have a better idea or suggestion, you can visit the "Cool Time" Web site at www.cool-time.com.

What Does the Title Mean?
The terms "Cool Time" and "the two-pound bucket" represent two of the 12 principles upon which this book is founded. Each of these 12 principles offers insight into a particular area of time

management and is represented by a "figurehead," a metaphor or image that acts as its symbol. An actual two-pound bucket, for example, stands for the notion of refining your actions within time, whereas an I-Beam stands for "planning and structure."

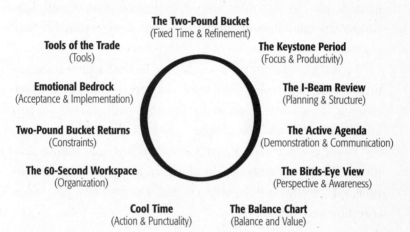

The Two-Pound Bucket
(Fixed Time & Refinement)

Tools of the Trade
(Tools)

The Keystone Period
(Focus & Productivity)

Emotional Bedrock
(Acceptance & Implementation)

The I-Beam Review
(Planning & Structure)

Two-Pound Bucket Returns
(Constraints)

The Active Agenda
(Demonstration & Communication)

The 60-Second Workspace
(Organization)

The Birds-Eye View
(Perspective & Awareness)

Cool Time
(Action & Punctuality)

The Balance Chart
(Balance and Value)

After the figurehead, each chapter then expands into practical, personal techniques that will help you apply time management skills to real-world situations. These are immediately useful actions — things that you can implement right away — such as holding time-effective meetings, dealing with distractions, learning to focus, coping with unrealistic workloads, and negotiating with your manager over conflicting tasks. There are even suggestions on important non-work activities, such as planning your vacation and enjoying a leisurely breakfast.

Finally, perspective is added to each chapter to help explain why we continually seem to have problems in this particular area, and why the application of each time management principle is so very important for our personal well-being and productivity.

Each of the figureheads and their related personal techniques coordinate with the other principles and techniques very well, and if you investigate them all, you will find that, together, they form a powerful unit. However, if you prefer to pick just one or two and work solely with them, this is equally possible, since each principle is capable of standing on its own. I invite you to read all 12 principles, in any order that your schedule permits, and then choose the combination and pattern that best fit your life and priorities.

What if you don't have enough time to read a time management book? Then don't. At least, don't read the whole thing at once. This book respects the fact that your time is already limited. That is why the chapters are kept short, independent, and to the point. If you currently need guidance on dealing with procrastination or workaholism, for example, you'll find subsections specifically on those subjects, ready and waiting (the index will show you where).

You Can Do It!

Some of the procedures and suggestions presented here may seem radical, especially in the context of your current corporate culture. Putting them into practice may appear strange to your co-workers or family. Part of this book's mandate, therefore, is to help you to maintain confidence and vision as you identify your time wasters and steer yourself back on course. Though we all live in an increasingly fast-paced environment, your life will always be different from that of your neighbor, and your time management solutions must be yours and yours alone. This book allows you to tailor your solutions accordingly and attain success through vision, perseverance, judgment, and organization.

1

The Two-Pound Bucket: Fixed Time and Refinement

Imagine for a moment that you are standing in my yard, and there is a bucket on a table in front of you. The bucket is gray, made of tin, and weighs about two pounds. Now suppose I was to inform you that your task for the day is to clean up the yard, and that the only tool you'll have to work with is that bucket. There are all kinds of building materials to be moved, there's a trench filled with rainwater, and there are some valuable and rather fragile flowers that must be re-planted.

Where to start? The flowers are beginning to wilt a little in the sun. The gardener who planted the flowers claims they are part of a prize-winning collection, and they need urgent attention. The rainwater in the trench, however, is starting to seep into the basement, and I'm not pleased about that. The building materials consist of bricks, gravel, and sand, and must be cleared from the yard by the end of today. And to compound it all, the yard is enclosed by a fence, with neighbors' yards on all sides, so throwing things over the fence is out of the question.

Perhaps you should start by emptying the trench of rainwater, given the importance I have placed on this particular task. But how? You could fill the bucket to the absolute top, but could you not also place a few of the flowers in the bucket with the rainwater? This would start to get them out of the way and perhaps revive them at the same time.

Alternatively, you could start to fill the bucket by locating an armload of bricks, which you could place carefully, one by one, into the bucket until they reached the top. But given the amount of work ahead of you, it would be wise to conserve energy by reducing the number of trips taken. What if you were to place small stones in the gaps between the bricks? You would probably be able to place a good number of stones into those spaces before finally reaching the rim of the bucket. What about sand? If you were to scoop up a few large handfuls of sand from the ground, you could pour the sand down into the bucket, shaking it a couple of times to get it all the way to the bottom. More sand could be poured around the bricks and the stones until the sand becomes level with the top of the bucket.

Would it be wiser, instead, to mix the sand and rainwater together, since mud would be a more stable cargo, especially if you were to hoist the bucket on your shoulder to reduce the strain on your hands?

Or perhaps it would be best to turn the empty bucket upside down, so as to be able to stand on it and see if there is anyone on the other side of the fence whom you could recruit to share the burden.

The level of success you attain on this day depends not so much on the sheer effort of your work, but on the amount of time you take in stepping back and assessing the tasks in front of you. It's about learning how to use the bucket most effectively, rather than simply wishing for a bigger one.

The two-pound bucket represents a fixed volume of time. We all have a two-pound bucket — every one of us, every day. We each have access to a 24-hour-long container, a vessel for the efforts of our lives. We get a new one each day, but we can't borrow any volume from previous days' buckets, nor can we ask for repeats or advances. These 24-hour containers come and go, regularly and unfailingly. The bucket is fixed in size and volume. It is the primary working tool of our existence.

The trick to time management, just like the trick to clearing the yard, is in learning how to fill your bucket rather than trying to find a bigger one. Time management comes from strategy, from an awareness of the value of every minute of the day, not by making more work hours available or by working twice as fast or twice as hard. Effective time managers do not feel an obsessive need to fill every moment with productive work — quite the opposite. They envision and enact a rational plan to fill every moment with valuable, quality time. They balance priorities. They recognize that the inbox will never actually empty, and they accept that. They go home at the end of the day knowing that good work has been performed, and that more will be done tomorrow.

If you find yourself constantly wishing for more hours in a day, what you're really doing is searching for a bigger bucket. The problem here is that even with a bigger bucket, you'll still end up working twice as hard to move half as much stuff. The art of time management is the art of refining time, locating those pockets of wasted time, strategically prioritizing instead of plunging in headlong, and recognizing that constraints are no impediment to increased efficiency and satisfaction.

Changing your perception of time in this manner is not so straightforward. It demands that you defy convention and place yourself in the planner's role. It requires that you break free of the traditional perception that time is an uncontrollable force in which we are but passive observers. Such a change in attitude does not come easily.

Take a look, for example, at the way in which we refer to the sun. For centuries now, we have lived with the knowledge that the earth orbits the sun and not vice versa, yet in our day-to-day parlance we still refer to the sun as "coming up," "setting," or "passing behind a cloud." It is comfortable and traditional, yet it is inaccurate. Convention and reality often do not coincide.

With regards to time, society fills its vernacular with phrases that enliven time and make it a real commodity. Sayings such as "I haven't got the time," or "time flies," or "where did the day go?" give time an elastic realism that just isn't there. We talk about people "wasting time," "spending time," "killing time," as if it were a substance to be bought, sold, and reused. Everyone knows these are harmless sayings, but they stand at the foundation of ineffective time management by placing the blame and the responsibility for change squarely on the shoulders of time itself — shoulders that don't exist. We, as individuals, are the ones who must instead embrace the challenge of understanding and controlling our actions within time.

Rhythm and circularity are the chief villains in this "active time" scenario. Part of the reason time is given such a dynamic role in our lives is because time markers such as hours, days, and months, as well as cultural markers including Christmas, Hanukkah, and Ramadan, seem to "come around" at their appointed intervals when really we, the humans, are advancing upon them like ants marching along a ruler.

The human relationship to rhythm is not a quirk, but a physiological reality. We pick up on rhythms subconsciously in accordance with our makeup as living organisms. Many aspects of our existence are based on rhythms: our beating heart is but one of numerous rhythmic patterns in the human body. The continued rotations of days, nights, seasons, tides, and the moon all come to us without fail. The plants and trees of the world breathe and release carbon dioxide every 24 hours, while large-scale weather patterns ferry moisture, cold, and warmth from one part of the globe to another. The planet itself seems to be breathing, living, and playing to its own vast cadence.

It is no surprise, therefore, that we humans, patently aware of our surroundings, have chosen to delineate time with the same characteristics and rhythms as the bodies and environments we call our home.

The two-pound bucket, then, is a metaphor to help us counter the illusion that time is dispensable just because it renews itself every 24 hours. It is impossible and impractical to remove rhythm from our calendar, so instead we must focus on refining both our attitudes to, and our use of, the time we have available.

As you start to integrate the time management techniques offered in the following sections of this book, do so with the attitude that success comes not from stretching the day — either by wishing for more hours, or by working late into every evening — but from refining the fixed amount of time available. Use planning, prioritization, delegation, and efficient work habits to approach your tasks in the right order, to fill in the gaps of wasted time, and to remain aware that it takes more than just bricks to fill a two-pound bucket.

2

The Keystone Period:
Focus and Productivity

A Keystone Period is a block of undisturbed work time that ranges from 30 minutes to two hours. An efficient time manager makes sure to build a Keystone Period into every day, or at least four days out of five. It is probably the single most useful technique for maximizing efficiency and refining time, since two hours of undisturbed work will yield greater productivity than the same number of minutes' worth of work spread throughout an entire day.

What do you do during your Keystone Period? You work on whatever you have decided to be the most important, highest priority task of the day. As best as you can, you avoid answering the phone, receiving visitors, and catering to distractions. You simply focus on, and work on, your number-one priority task.

This makes good sense because the human brain enjoys focusing. In fact, multitasking, a term that finds itself at the heart of many job descriptions, is a physical impossibility — and, as such, leads to unrealistic expectations about productivity and time management. Your conscious brain operates in a manner similar to the computer you have on your desk. Even with its amazing speed and versatility, it can pay attention to only one item at a time. Sure, you may have a dozen things on the go, but only one of them can be in focus at any given moment. The only multitasking of which you are truly capable happens on the inside, thanks to your autonomic ability to digest breakfast, ferry oxygen through your bloodstream, and keep all of your systems in equilibrium — all while you type your report or drive to work.

While in the Keystone Period, your duty is to focus your physical and mental energies on what you have determined to be your highest priority. This is work — real work, pure productivity. You cannot, and should not, maintain this level of focus and concentration throughout the entire day. In fact, attempting to do so can yield inferior results. This is a short-spell, high-impact achievement device.

Working within a Keystone Period in this way will not only guarantee a rise in your productivity and efficiency, but it will also help you feel terrific. The satisfaction gleaned from the knowledge that you have attained your day's goal, especially if you do so before lunch, provides a subconscious boost that drives you forward while helping to alleviate some of the day's stresses. Everything else you achieve after a Keystone Period feels like a bonus. It enables you to go home each night at a reasonable time while your mind reflects on, and basks in, the glow of the day's achievements, rather than on unfinished business.

Here is a sample day schedule that includes a Keystone Period. It doesn't take up much space, just a quarter of an eight-hour workday.

7:00

8:00

9:00   9:00–11:00 Keystone Period: Work on ABC Report

10:00

11:00

12:00

1:00

2:00

3:00

4:00

5:00

6:00

Making the Keystone Period Work

Success in using a Keystone Period starts with its placement in your calendar: one for every day of this week, next week, and the week after that. Sure, as the days go by you may have to reschedule one or two of them to make room for other activities, but that's OK. They do not have to occur at the same time every day. The important thing is to have one scheduled for each day, most days of the week. This is where your top-priority task will be dealt with and completed.

What if you don't yet know what your top-priority task will be for a particular day? No matter. Create the space for it now. You will be able to fill in the actual task later.

Visibility Equals Reality

By physically entering a daily Keystone Period into your calendar as a scheduled appointment, you are setting aside space for productive, important work. Your Keystone Period now becomes a clearly defined task in and of itself. This is a great psychological step beyond simply being aware that you have "work to do." The physically scheduled Keystone Period makes the "work block" real, rather than leaving it as a vague concept inside your head.

Your Personal Parking Space at the Mall

Think of the number of times you've set out somewhere, perhaps to a shopping mall or downtown, only to find your plans have to be delayed while you circle the block or cruise the parking lot looking for a space. It takes the momentum out of your trip, at least for a short while, yet it's something we usually don't think about until we arrive. Wouldn't it be nice to have a permanent, personal parking space to just slide into whenever we want?

Private parking spaces are one of the perks that come with corporate promotions, and for good reason. They allow your time to be spent on your tasks (the reason for your travels), rather than on the travel itself.

By creating Keystone Periods in advance, you are creating parking spaces for the important work yet to come. Without them, your day will fill up with odd tasks and distractions, and the time you waste "circling" – trying to find time in an already crowded day – becomes wasteful and irretrievable.

When a colleague asks if you are available for a meeting or some other event that distracts and detracts from your priority list, it is a lot easier to say "no" and to offer him/her an alternate date if you actually have a real event (your Keystone Period) occupying the time slot in question.

Deflect Lesser Activities

As I discuss in Chapter 4, one of the secrets to time management success — and a key ingredient in refining your allotted time —

is to identify your number-one task and then do it. Many people are already able to identify their most important task, yet they allow distractions, meetings, and less important items to get in the way. And yes, some meetings are important, but many are also wasteful, overly long, and not structured for optimal use of people's time. By reserving an hour or two every day for whatever you decide your top priority will be, you will be able to work on the task that holds the greatest value to you. Having part of your daily calendar already filled by the Keystone Period gives you a lever — the power to exert influence over the timing of secondary events such as meetings, so as to allow them to surround — not replace — your productive working time.

Optimize Your Day

A lot of time management problems stem from people trying to do too many tasks in a day without assigning realistic durations to them. A dose of reality should be included here. It is very often the case that you simply can't do all the things that you want to do in any given day, and the tasks you do undertake will take longer than desired. Tasks of lesser importance, as well as the ever-present task of returning calls and e-mail, end up getting spread across the whole of the available workday, stepping into your field of view and obscuring your vision. Trying to deal with tasks simply in the order they arrive is like herding cats. You'll never get them all in line and they'll all claim to be the most important. The Keystone Period helps to keep you focused on your most important task, keeping all the others at bay until you're ready to approach them in a logical, time-efficient sequence.

Your computer can serve as a role model for you in this instance.

This image represents part of a computer's hard drive after heavy usage. The dark sections represent used spaces, while the light sections are unused. When a computer saves data, the files are deposited anywhere on the disk that is convenient, which results in a patchwork quilt of used and unused spaces. Though many unused spaces remain, they are small, far apart, and unable to save large amounts of data. When this happens, it becomes necessary to "optimize" or "defragment" the drive in order to redistribute the used and unused blocks, increasing storage capacity and efficiency.

This second image represents the same computer's hard drive after being optimized. Used and unused blocks are grouped and sent to their respective corners, so as to allow more information to be stored in exactly the same amount of storage space. Sound familiar? That's the principle behind the two-pound bucket, and it's what effective planning and time management are all about: optimizing your schedule to allow better use of time and energy without requiring extra hours. Does it take time to do this? Yes, sure. It takes a while to optimize a hard drive, and it takes a few minutes to plan your day. It takes a few minutes to identify your number-one task and to schedule a Keystone Period. Is it worth it? In both cases, absolutely yes.

Be Flexible

If higher-priority events, or events over which you have no control, actually do take precedence, it is easy to reschedule your Keystone Period to a different part of the day. Take care to *reschedule*, however, rather than delete it. Though a particular meeting or client may take top priority under certain circumstances, the scheduling and maintenance of your Keystone Period, and the completion of the task assigned to it, must remain a top priority on an ongoing basis.

Encouraging Focus

When your mind becomes aware that there is only a fixed amount of time to get something done, it is more apt to focus its energy than if you just plan to "work until it's finished." Clearly defined start and end times are akin to a short foot race in which the finish line is already in view. In both cases, you are targeting and consolidating your energies, with a precisely measured amount of time in which to spend them.

An Antidote to "Answerholism"

We are besieged daily by e-mail, voice mail, postal mail, phone calls, and other communications, and for numerous reasons, we feel obliged to answer these calls for attention the moment they happen. The concept of a Keystone Period can be difficult to accept in the face of such technological persistence, since an undisturbed block of time means *not* answering incoming calls and mail immediately.

To increase the strain, communications technologies seem to bring with them their own sense of urgency and mystery. They beep, ring, vibrate, or pop up messages on your screen to alert you to their presence. They demand to be answered. It is difficult to resist taking a call, reading a message, or checking your e-mail, since the next one may be the big one. It might even be urgent! It's an overwhelming sensation.

I refer to this urge as "answerholism," and it becomes counterproductive as reflex overtakes perspective.

Take, for example, your phone. Why must you answer the phone? For some professionals, such as receptionists and customer service staff, this is an easy question to answer: it is part of the job description and must be dealt with immediately. For others, however, the urge to answer the phone simply springs from habit, curiosity, and/or a sense of obligation.

There's no question that answering the phone is important. My suggestion, however, is that *when* you answer the phone is equally important. The interruptions caused by a phone call erode your capacity for concentration and clear thought. Every time you take a call, your subconscious mind loses momentum. It takes between six and 20 minutes for your mind to return to the level of intensity and concentration it enjoyed before the call. Can you put a dollar figure on that?

Successful time management involves being able to ignore all but the highest priority phone calls and e-mails until after the Keystone Period. That's all. Just for an hour or two. Most things can wait that long. Get your high-priority Keystone work done properly, and leave the communications stuff until afterwards. Give them their own time slots: use message-returning periods.

Message-Returning Periods

Since your Keystone Period is an interval in which no calls or e-mail are attended to, it is necessary to schedule times during the day in which communication happens. These are your message-returning periods. Assign one, two, or three of these periods into your day specifically for reading e-mail, listening to voice mail, and returning messages. Consider these message-returning periods as fixed appointments. If you estimate that you currently require two hours or more out of each day to return calls, and these calls comprise a major part of your job, then plan an hour in the late morning after your Keystone Period, half an hour after lunch, and an hour in the late afternoon. This now becomes part of your scheduled day.

It doesn't take long to discover that your day quickly fills up: a Keystone Period, followed by a message-returning period, lunch, a second message-returning period, a meeting, a third message-returning period, and pretty soon, it's 5:00. Some people are dismayed at this. "Where is the time for my project or my conference call?" they ask. "How can I fit all the rest of my duties in?"

Well, this is what effective time management is all about: you block your day into components of maximized productivity rather than answering each call as it comes in. You focus your effort, rather than succumbing to distraction, by completing one task at a time instead of continually picking up the fractured remains of your efforts after each interruption. You recognize and accept that e-mail and voice mail are as much a part of your job as any other task, but that they must be scheduled accordingly. You optimize your day. You take control.

Here is a sample day schedule that includes a Keystone Period, to which we add three message-returning periods:

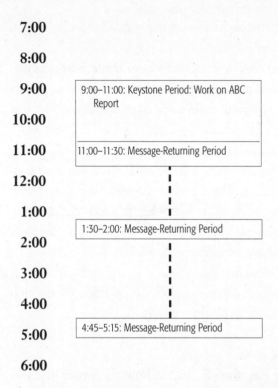

Notice there's still space available for meetings, for your conference call, for other work, and even for a healthy lunch.

Put Some Weekend into Your Weekday

David Nelson, a personal productivity speaker from Tampa, Florida, recounts this great analogy of how a good weekend illustrates the value that blocks of focused time can bring. Imagine how your weekend would look, he states, if you ran it like a typical business day: you start the lawn mower, walk six feet, then leave the mower, run downstairs, and hammer a few nails into the workbench you're building. Then you run upstairs, pick up a paintbrush, apply a few strokes of paint to the wall in the second bedroom, run back outside to your still-running mower, cut six more feet of grass, run back upstairs, apply some more paint, run downstairs, and so on.

It doesn't make sense to work that way at home, and the same applies at work. Time management is about focusing your efforts and resisting the temptation to cater to every distraction just because it's there.

YES. BUT... People often think they will be perceived as inaccessible or unprofessional if they do not answer their e-mail or phone calls right away. However, provided that you actually stick to your scheduled message-returning periods, your clients and colleagues will learn that you are really very accessible and reliable. Their calls will be returned promptly, within an hour or two — an acceptable delay in all but the highest priority and extreme cases. This practice will establish an impressive precedent for others to match.

Set Some Ground Rules
To implement the Keystone Period and optimize your day, you need to set some ground rules that you and your colleagues must follow. Doing this can be tricky, since it requires changing the status quo, a topic that I'll expand upon in the next chapter. It requires that you "train" your colleagues, clients, and superiors to understand and respect your terms of work — and that is something that most of us are not inclined to do. But ground rules need not be officious, antisocial, or anti-establishment. They are there simply to guide you and your co-workers toward a positive, productive, and healthy work relationship. Most people would agree that a parking lot with no lines painted on it would soon devolve into a jumble of cars, conflicts, and wasted space. That's all I'm suggesting here: painting some lines — applying guidance and structure to the surface of the workday.

Keep Your "Door" Closed

Make it clear to colleagues that you are unavailable for the duration of your Keystone Period. If you have an office with a real door, closing it is a lot easier than if you work in a cubicle, but even in this latter case the closed-door policy can still be applied. The objective is to eliminate distractions and focus entirely on the work you have assigned yourself. The "door" in both instances, whether office or cubicle, really refers to a temporary barrier between you and the people around you. For that brief hour or two during your Keystone Period, you must close yourself off.

YES, BUT... Are you responsible to other staff members? Does your job keep you constantly "on call"? Would closing your door fly in the face of your current management objectives of being approachable and responsible? Of course it feels that way. But remember, the Keystone Period lasts only for a short while, maybe an hour, maybe two. You wouldn't be closing the door on your staff for an entire day or week. It is possible and justifiable to allow yourself some time during each day to focus on top-priority work, yet remain available and approachable for your colleagues and subordinates the rest of the day. (I'll discuss this principle in more detail later in this chapter.)

Entertain No Visitors

When you are involved in top-priority Keystone Period work, don't allow people to drop in. Don't converse with passers-by. Don't make eye contact. Don't allow anyone to interrupt your train of thought. Distractions not only stop you from doing what you are supposed to be doing, but they make it very difficult for your mind to return to the level of concentration it enjoyed before the interruption. This loss of concentration is expensive.

23

It costs you time. Of course, fending off interruptions is not easy, and should be done carefully and within the context of your workplace culture. But it is here that many people fall off the time management wagon. They find that they simply cannot fend off the distractions of the day. (Suggestions for delicately deflecting visitors are provided later in this chapter.)

Schedule No Meetings

If you have any input into the times that meetings are scheduled, make sure they're set for a time other than your Keystone Period. If you have no say whatsoever in meeting times, then move your Keystone Period around to make sure your day plan includes the meeting *and* a Keystone Period. Remember, a Keystone Period does not have to occur at the same time every day, but you should ensure you have one each day. I've already mentioned how having a Keystone Period marked in your calendar is a powerful method of defining available time, and this may come in handy when the memo comes around asking "Are you available Tuesday morning?" You may also be able to influence the way in which meetings are run, perhaps by helping them to start and end on time — thus allowing you to return to what is truly important. (You can find more information about running effective meetings in Chapter 3.)

Avoid Temptation

Temptation is self-generated distraction. It consists of those things that call us away from the tasks at hand and then gnaw away at our time with no appreciable gain. After the temptation has passed, the real work still remains. When you are hard at work in your Keystone Period, cast aside all of those extraneous activities that you feel the urge to address. Remind yourself that a better time for them exists. If mail arrives, don't look at it. If Internet research is part of your Keystone Period work, avoid the temptation to visit sites that are not related to your tasks. The phone? Let voice mail take it. If you have a call-display phone, it makes sense to briefly check, just in case the caller is "top-priority," but let everyone else use your voice mail. Whereas distractions are external, coming from your immediate environment, temptation comes from within. It must be countered diligently, by reminding yourself of the value of your Keystone Period, the importance of achieving your goal for the day. Bribe yourself with whatever is important: the vision of making that sale, finalizing that project, going home on time.

Don't Leave Your Desk

Make sure you have your coffee and/or water before you start your Keystone Period. Don't go for photocopies or any other supplies. Keep yourself at your desk for the duration of the Keystone Period. Why? Because once you leave your desk, you set yourself up for further distraction and delay in the form of the "Hallway Ambush." It is inevitable, whether you work in an office or at home, that a trip to the kitchen, washroom, or anywhere else will lead to encounters, distraction, and delay. If people see you, they'll want to talk. If you need to take an elevator, you'll have to wait for it. As soon as you move around, distractions will occur. The hallway ambush is a notorious swallower of time, one that we often overlook in the name of being civil, cooperative, and approachable to our colleagues. Remember, the Keystone Period is about uninterrupted, focused work, and it comprises only a small portion of your day. There will be time later for interaction, after the Keystone Period is done.

YES, BUT... "That will never work here!" is the common response when the Keystone Period is introduced to people for the first time. They point out that there's just too much going on, and that "disappearing" for two hours would not be good for one's performance review and one's career. Well, if a two-hour block is impossible, then consider two one-hour blocks, or maybe just one one-hour block, or two blocks of 45 minutes. The length of the Keystone Period is up to you. The point is to find some time throughout the course of the business day in which you can focus and complete your highest priority task. It really works, people will still be able to find you and talk to you throughout the rest of the day, and above all, it is a matter of survival.

Maximizing Focus and Productivity

In our circle of the 12 "Cool Time" principles, the Keystone Period stands as the figurehead for a set of time management techniques that contribute to "focus and productivity," the art of getting things done and done right. Here, then, are some additional suggestions for ensuring that your time is well spent.

Work in Short Blocks

The ability to concentrate on a single task to the exclusion of all other stimuli is a practiced art. It does not come naturally to most people, since our senses — sight, hearing, touch, taste, and smell — together with active conscious thought, cause us to veer from one item to another very quickly. And true focus can be quite tiring — it takes a lot of energy to stay singular of mind. In the physical world, if you stay in one position too long, parts of you will start to go numb, since muscles and bones need constant movement. The same applies to our mental selves. Any attempt to stay focused for extended periods of time will eventually result in reduced concentration, and will bring on either frustration, distraction, a reduction in work quality, or the desire to sleep.

This means that the Keystone Period itself should be divided into segments of concentration and rest, with an emphasis on avoiding outside distractions. In the context of a workday, the Keystone Period is a block of undisturbed time, yet within that block, it really helps to give your mental muscles a break.

Allow yourself focus periods of 20 or 30 minutes in which you work solidly and diligently. Then, take a two-minute break. Look up. Look around. Allow your eyes to change their focus. Stand up. Stretch. Or, if standing up in a cubicle poses too much of a risk of being seen — and therefore being intruded upon — do a few chair-based stretches, including reaching toward the ceiling and stretching your arms fully outwards, to stretch the rib cage and the upper back.

Gather All the Things You'll Need — Eliminate Those You Don't

Before you start your focus period, ensure that all your files, disks, notes, and other materials are available and within your line of sight. Focus is about working on what is in front of you, not searching the office for things that are missing.

Remove from your field of view any documents, memos, or items that refer to other projects. Also, turn off the ringer on your phone and close down your e-mail software. (If you can't close it down, then disable the "new e-mail" alert feature.) Your objective here is to have all that you need and none of what you don't need within your field of view.

Get Comfortable

Kick off your shoes. Make sure your chair is the right height and spine and feet are properly supported. Get your computer monitor, keyboard, and mouse aligned to your forearms, wrist, and line of sight. Get your refreshments lined up, and if you drink coffee or tea, definitely balance this out with water. Caffeine, in addition to being a stimulant (which can be useful), is also a diuretic, which will dehydrate you quickly, impairing concentration and increasing the need to attend to the call of nature.

Make sure you have correct lighting. If your office suffers from a lack of natural light, there are specialty desk- and monitor-mounted lamps available that reproduce the light spectrum found outdoors and help counteract the glare and flicker found on many computer monitors.

Invest in a Squeeze Ball

Since our physical bodies need constant movement and stimulation, this energy must be channeled during periods of focus; it cannot be dammed up. The best tool for this is a simple sponge squeeze ball. You can buy one from an office supply store or a toy store. It is a practical and inexpensive stress reducer and energy channeler. In addition to squeezing it with your hand, you can also channel energy by rolling the ball between your feet or between your knees. The important point is to allow a constant release of energy as a counterbalance to your intense concentration.

Master the Follow-Through

If you've ever played golf, or even watched it on TV, you will undoubtedly be aware of the importance of the "follow-through." Even after the ball has been hit and is on its way toward the green, the player must still focus on proper form, swing, and balance. What possible effect could this have on a ball that has left the tee and is no longer under the player's control?

28

Follow-through is not an independent action: it is the end phase of a series of actions that started with "addressing the ball," and continued through the motion of swinging the club for an appropriate stroke. Without a planned and practiced follow-through, all of the actions that preceded it would yield inferior results and the player would be at a disadvantage.

In the day-to-day world, every task, every action you perform should be planned first, and then followed through to a clearly defined end. Our temptation, however, is to simply get "stuck in," to start on a task with little thought given to the sequence of events required, not to mention their impact on other tasks. We bow to a very real pressure to get started, to demonstrate our commitment, to soothe our consciences, and to look good in the eyes of our superiors. Such reactions are honest and earnest in their motivation, but they also invite error and delay.

The follow-through approach to focus and productivity draws from the pages of project management theory rather than golf school. Project management emphasizes planning, control, and communication as elements necessary for success in a project. Since every task you, as an individual, undertake contributes either to a specific project within your company or, more generally, to the projects you call your day, your week, your year, and your life, it makes sense to put on a project manager's hat and view your tasks with an eye to successful project completion.

The basic follow-through procedure encompasses project management principles through the following four steps (project management itself is described in more detail in Chapter 4).

1. *Plan*

Visualize the task from beginning to end. Planning is everything. It allows you to define the task at hand, visualize it in your mind's eye through to its completion, and anticipate problems that may crop up. Every time a task is presented to you, go through this process. Make sure to run through the task from beginning to end before undertaking it.

Project managers are taught the absolute importance of planning at the outset. But to an outside observer, the act of planning does not look like action at all. Someone engaged in the act of planning is thinking and visualizing. Rather than grabbing a shovel and starting to dig, the person is exploring the life of the project in his or her mind's eye.

It is not wrong to spend a large proportion of the life of a project doing nothing but planning, but many project managers are afraid of this. They feel that if their manager sees them just sitting around and that no work appears to have yet been done, then they will be seen as lazy or incompetent.

However, without planning, projects quickly go over budget, over time, and into deep trouble. It is extremely rare that "seat-of-the-pants" management brings in a project satisfactorily. For both multi-week projects and simpler tasks, there is nothing wrong in taking the time to plan — in fact, it is the best thing you can do.

You may think, "Sure, planning makes sense when I have a big project coming up, but I don't need to formally plan to make a phone call, do I?" The answer is yes, you do, but in miniature. No phone call should be taken or made without the proper documents at hand and a point-form list of the items to be discussed. This is especially useful when dealing with voice mail, in which concise, clear messages can move a project along without delay.

2. *Perform*

Once you have your project plan committed to paper, it is time to perform the task. Try to get the task done with as few interruptions as possible. If a task is too large to be done in one session, make sure to end on a "milestone": a clearly defined end point of work, like the end of a chapter in a book. Whenever possible, however, seek to complete the task in one go. The more often an action is interrupted, the longer it will take to complete, and when momentum is broken, it takes a long time to rebuild. A task that is interrupted will take longer in elapsed time than a non-interrupted task.

3. *Follow Through*
Once the task has been performed, it's time for the follow-through. Following through on an activity helps set the stage for subsequent tasks. For a simple phone call, this may include

- entering notes about the call into the appropriate file, either on paper or on your computer;
- scheduling a follow-up call;
- noting and scheduling the tasks you promised to undertake in your phone conversation; and
- noting and scheduling the tasks promised by the other party.

Most people never get to the follow-through phase. As soon as the phone receiver is put back, they move on to the next task of the day, forgetting to note the follow-ups, forgetting to record the points made in the call, and forgetting to clearly mark the next step in the project. Maybe they intend to get these things done at the end of the day, or maybe they're just counting on storing the information mentally, to be recorded whenever there's time. This is where things fall between the cracks.

Each task must have a follow-through. Whether you are working on a report or cooking a meal, the activity isn't over until things are put away, follow-up tasks are planned, and the next phase of the task is clearly understood. Follow-through guarantees continuity in terms of achievement and in terms of understanding where this particular project is taking you. There is no task too small for a follow-through.

4. *Acknowledge*

Acknowledge your achievement. Every activity, from a Keystone Period to a meeting to a return phone call, should be entered into your schedule and then crossed off once it has been completed. Studies have shown that recognizing the completion of a task by crossing it off does a number of good things:

- It gives psychological validation that the task is now over and allows the mind to focus on the next task.
- It demonstrates achievement.
- It creates a written record of your work.

It feels good to cross things out. The manufacturers of day planners, both paper-based and software-based, encourage their users to cross off completed tasks rather than erase them.

Crossing out or checking off also gives the effective time manager one last chance to ask, "Was everything completed for this task? Has it been properly followed through?"

This project-management-based, four-step process for completing a task forces you to redefine the definition of that task. It ensures that work is not limited to the doing of a task, but also includes the planning beforehand and follow-through afterward. Following this process may be a difficult habit to get into, but it allows all tasks to be completed and accounted for. It eliminates time wasted in preparing for, or even determining, the follow-up events at a later time. It thwarts forgetfulness and enhances efficiency, and as such makes up one of the central tenets of time management.

Eliminate Distractions

When I ask people about the biggest obstacles they face in improving their "focus and productivity" techniques, distractions always land on top of the pile. Distractions pull people away from the tasks they should be doing and cloud the air with confusion and diversion. Like gremlins, they poke and pull at the fabric of your day, diluting your efforts, and leaving stress and frustration in their wake. They come in two forms: those that you are aware of and those that distract to such a degree that you don't realize until later that you've been distracted. They can be delivered either by the people in your immediate sphere or by the events that surround you.

The best way to counteract distractions is to avoid them. Don't allow yourself to get sidetracked. Learn to politely say "No." Keep your true goals and priorities for the day clearly in sight. Remember that it's your time that's at stake. Here are some examples:

When People Distract

When people are the source of your distraction, the dilemma for the effective time manager is how to maintain an appearance of approachability while not becoming a habitual victim of time theft. This balancing act is difficult. Our desire to appear available, effective, enthusiastic, and approachable forces us to inversely prioritize — to place the needs of our colleagues before our own. We often do this without thinking. We do it to be polite, or simply to blend in with the existing corporate culture.

We let it happen to us, because there seems to be no other way. Well, forget it! It's time to use the "intelligent push-back" to retaliate against time theft and place your priorities first.

The intelligent push-back is a technique for saying "no" without being hurtful or self-defeating, and it runs through the whole of the Cool Time philosophy. In this case, when we apply it as a barrier to distractions, it does not mean severing all contacts with your colleagues. After all, teamwork and social interaction within a corporate setting are important, and should not be ignored or suppressed. But realistically, there's only so much you can do in a day, and taking on more will jeopardize everything. Think back to the Two-Pound Bucket. If it's already filled to the brim with water, any amount extra that you try to put in will result in an equal amount running right back out again. When a distraction starts to happen, make sure to keep your priorities in mind. Keep your personal productivity and personal availability in careful, thoughtful balance. It takes practice and tact to make this work effectively, but you don't have to become a grouch or a social outcast for it to be successful. Here are a few examples.

A colleague sticks his or her head in the door and says, "Have you got a minute?" What do you say? If you respond to this question by saying, "Sure, come on in, what can I do for you?" you may think you're saying, "I'm approachable and capable. I'm a good professional," but what you're actually saying is, "Sure, your time is more valuable than mine — go ahead and use up as much as you want." You are allowing a visitor's time and priorities to take precedence over your own. As soon as you allow someone to chisel into your block of time, you are giving up things that cannot be won back.

Let's look at the sources of internal conflict that this distraction-situation presents: You don't want to actually engage this person in a conversation — you're already too busy. But neither would you want to cause anger or hurt feelings in rejecting this person outright. Also, you don't want to appear unapproachable or unfriendly to the office community, yet it wouldn't be wise to set a precedent in which anyone and everyone will drop in to see you at any time. And of course, a "minute" never actually takes a minute. So, what can you do? Part of the intelligent push-back in a situation like this involves the "deflect-and-save-face" technique:

When a colleague wants a moment of your time right away, provide him/her with an alternate time for the discussion. An answer to the original question, "Have you got a minute?" would therefore sound like this: "Well, at the moment I'm in the middle of this work, but I will come to see you at 11:15." In this way you are guaranteeing the interrupter your undivided attention at a later time, not too far away. You are demonstrating respect for your colleague's concerns, and most importantly you are helping that person "save face" by deflecting him/her from your current activities without being insulting. It is crucial, however, that you follow up on your promise in this scenario. If you say 11:15, then you must visit your colleague at that time.

Incidentally, whenever you use this technique, make a habit of becoming the visitor rather than inviting your colleague to return to your workspace at 11:15. Why? Whenever you make the visitation, you are at liberty to end it whenever you want — you remain in control. When the visitor comes to you, getting him or her to leave your workspace in a timely manner may become a challenge.

Culturally, the deflect-and-save-face technique may seem odd, especially if no one else in the office does it. But stick with it! Provide people with alternative times to talk and follow up on those promises. Soon you will develop a reputation for being accessible and approachable, even though you are doing it on your own terms!

If you think the deflect-and-save-face technique is truly unworkable, think of other professional people from whom this behavior is already expected: company presidents and senior officials, dentists, doctors, and lawyers. These types of people seldom have time for you the moment you call — they work by appointment. Wouldn't you be more than a little surprised, perhaps even a little concerned, if your own doctor answered the phone when you called? Making appointments to see the people who need to see you is a profitable and efficient use of your time. It demonstrates a professional talent for prioritization while maintaining approachability and accessibility with colleagues.

When employing the deflect-and-save-face technique as part of your intelligent push-back, be polite yet firm. It's not necessary to be mean or objectionable when declining a person's drop-in visit. "No" is a lot easier to pronounce when it is followed up with an alternative time for discussion:

Interrupter: Hi. Got a minute?

You: Not really, Bob. I'm just in the middle of this report, and I have half an hour left. How's 11:15 for you?

Don't feel you have to explain too much. If you answer "No" to the "Got a minute?" question, and then follow that up with too many specifics, such as "I'm working on the Johnson report right now," you are opening up a bargaining position in which the interrupter may assess the importance of the Johnson report against that of his own request — and then gain the upper hand by deciding his own request to be of higher priority for both of you, leaving you with little room to put forth a second objection. Volunteer no information that may serve to dilute your position.

Keep your agenda nearby and reachable. In those situations where you have no choice but to elaborate on why you don't have the time to entertain a visitor, your complete, up-to-date agenda demonstrates your schedule for the day in black and white, proving that you really are quite busy. It is far more credible than trying to recite a general description of your scheduled events from memory. (More information on maintaining an "Active Agenda" is available in Chapter 5).

Always handle your deflect-and-save-face response with care and discretion. Certain people, especially senior managers, may hold priorities that truly are higher than the work you are doing, and they therefore should be seen right away. Like all the suggestions in this book, use sensitivity and judgment in determining your priorities and framing your answers.

If, after all your best efforts, the visitor insists on speaking right then and there, allow the person a fixed amount of time — such as a minute or two — and stand up when his or her time is done. If the person still doesn't get the hint, make a move toward the door, to help "wrap up" the discussion. As polite as we all want to be, situations in which an interrupter's request is accommodated to your detriment rarely happen in isolation. It is dangerous, and very easy, to build a reputation as someone who can be visited at the convenience of the visitor. If people learn they can drop in on you at any time and spend as much time as they want, it will keep happening, and no work will get done.

Finally, don't allow interruptions to be a proxy for procrastination. Almost any diversion is welcome when you're faced with an undesirable task. Unfortunately, the task will still be there after your visitor has left, and all you'll have achieved is the loss of several minutes of your workday.

Sound Distractions

Since most people work in busy offices with little privacy, audible distractions are a major impediment to concentration and productivity. Many people find that moving to a different room is the best solution. An unused boardroom or office, especially one with a door, is a perfect setting for a productive Keystone Period. If a room is not available, consider using earplugs. They're inexpensive, discreet, effective, and can be purchased at any drugstore. They don't block out all sound — you would still be able to hear the fire alarm or the voice of somebody addressing you directly — but they drown out a great deal of background noise, especially the conversations of your colleagues.

A third option is to invest in noise-canceling headphones. Available at stereo stores or electronics shops, these headphones generate full-spectrum neutralization of background sound. As with earplugs, they do not render you deaf to alarms or direct voices, but instead create a quiet zone of audio isolation. Though some companies have policies forbidding the wearing of headphones at work, I believe there is justification in putting forth an argument to the effect that noise-canceling headphones do not fall into the same category as radio or CD-player headphones. They are, in terms of productivity and business-related use, on par with dictation headphones or telephone headsets.

Taking the Door out of Your "Open-Door" Policy

Whether you work in a corner office or a cubicle, a productive open-door policy should focus more on the word "policy" than on any physical door or entrance. An "open door" should remain an honest metaphor for accessibility and availability, but let's face it: you have work to do, too. In the previous section we looked at methods of dealing with an interrupter once this person already has his or her face in front of yours. But there's also a preemptive technique you can use to avoid such interrupters: post a schedule of "visiting hours" and stick to it. The trick is to let people know that you are certainly willing to make time for them, but "by appointment."

(YES, BUT..) "A schedule on the outside of my door? I can't do that. Corporate policy wouldn't allow it." That's the reaction most people have when first considering this principle. But a piece of paper on your front door or on the outside of your cubicle is not the only way to communicate your Keystone Period hours. Consider sending e-mail to staff members detailing your availability for the coming week, or printing your "available times" out on paper and handing it to visitors as you deflect and save face with them.

A visiting-hour list may not be common in an office environment, and at first glance it may seem to run counter to your culture of teamwork or *esprit de corps*. But it's neither as crazy nor as exclusive as it sounds. All I am really talking about is protecting the one or two hours per day that you wish to set aside as Keystone Period time. The rest of the time, you can be completely available if you wish, and as such you will then be able to give your visitors the attention they expect and deserve.

You can help "train" your colleagues by using Cool Time terminology in explaining your schedule. Show them you're unavailable because you're in your Keystone Period. Use that term. Start to "brand" your private, focused work time as a

Keystone Period, and help them associate that term with "do not disturb." And if they don't know what a Keystone Period is, explain it, including its benefits, using the printable explanation available on the cool-time.com Web site.

Accentuate the positive, as the song says, by emphasizing those blocks of time in which you are available. Take the focus away from the Keystone Period or other periods of unavailability, and guide your visitors' eyes to the rest of the day, in which complete communication is encouraged. The bottom line here is to make your schedule speak actively on your behalf, rather than just being a passive report. Give people a solid understanding of your posted schedule and, at the same time, let them know when they can see you. In this way you can maintain an open-door policy without becoming a doormat.

Finding Privacy in a Cubicle

In Chapter 6, I recount the results of a poll conducted at my time management seminars in which participants are invited to list the items that would constitute a "perfect workplace." One of the most popular and consistent requests is for an office with a door. Working people are crying out for privacy, and must deal daily with the sounds of other people's conversations, phone calls, and office activity, along with the visual distraction of people walking by (and possibly making eye contact), as well as the aroma of various types of lunch all floating over the low walls of our cubicles and gnawing away at our concentration and patience. Unfortunately, as long as the "open concept" work environment continues to be the chosen style of office interiors, we must work within its limitations, and privacy shall remain in short supply.

If possible, position your workstation in such a way as to avoid eye contact with passers-by. By and large, most cubicles are

arranged so that the computer or work area is at the side opposite the entrance, which allows you to turn your back somewhat
to passing traffic — a first step toward winning some privacy.

Send a message with your body language: "I am not to be
disturbed." Face inwards. If you are trying to think or trying to
talk on the phone, adopt a posture in which you avoid looking
outwards, catching other people's attention. Use your hands to
"blinker your vision": rest your elbows on the desk and place your
index fingers at your temples, with your hands aligned parallel to
your line of sight. This posture conveys a look of intense concentration, and as a bonus, it actually does help in concentrating.

As a privacy tool, these posture techniques work in three ways.
First, your closed posture tends to be less attractive to casual
passers-by, who merely want to make conversation. They will
be more inclined to move on to someone whose body language
is more inviting. Second, such a focused position may help dis-
courage others who are intent on talking to you, since most
people are reluctant to disturb people who are obviously busy.
This won't work on everybody of course, but it may help to cut
the interruptions down to some extent. Third, it helps you concentrate on what is really important. If you have a photograph or
two on your desk of your loved ones, make sure to keep them
within your field of view while in your "privacy posture." It will
help remind you why you are there in the first place, and why you
need to get home at a decent hour to be with them. It can be the
ultimate prioritization tool.

Once again, I propose that privacy can be found by outwardly
informing all passers-by that you are currently in your Keystone
Period and cannot be disturbed. This may seem at first like
bizarre behavior, but the point is that most people come to work
to perform a task and then get compensated for it. The social

interaction that comes from office life may be a pleasant perk, and is useful for maintaining a team atmosphere, but it must always be a complement to, not a replacement for productivity.

Finally, avoid being the instigator of a distracting environment. To prevent people from constantly dropping by your office to chat, make sure to avoid using your office for that purpose. This doesn't mean you have to become a hermit. What it does suggest is if you're the one who calls to a passing colleague, "Hey, Pat, did you see that show last night?", then your co-workers will soon learn that you and your cubicle are open for social interaction at any time. Stay friendly, of course, but stay aware of when and how you interact to avoid turning your workspace into a convivial stop-off between the kitchen and the washrooms.

Caution: All of these points should, of course, be taken with some moderation. Your work environment, a need to interact with colleagues, your desired level of concentration, and your professional responsibilities are but a few of the components that go into your specific workday. Some of these techniques may have to be introduced slowly into your office to avoid confusion or misunderstanding. Take it carefully, but be aware that you can do a lot more with your workday with just a little planning and some application.

3

The Galactic Rubber Floor Mat: Bending the Status Quo

Let's leave our earthly pursuits for a moment and think about one of the issues that dog scientists and astronomers: that of crossing impossibly large chasms of space in order to drop in on one of our galactic neighbors. The *light-year* is a term used to measure distances in space, and refers to how far light can travel in one solar year. Since light travels at approximately 186,000 miles (300,000 kilometers) per second, a light-year works out to about 5,880,000,000,000 miles (9,461,000,000,000 kilometers). Things are spaced so far apart out there that even light from the sun takes about eight minutes to reach Earth.

Traveling across galaxies therefore poses a monstrous time management challenge to those who would undertake it, in that the voyage would last much longer than any crew member's lifetime. But the gifted people who pursue quantum physics, such as Albert Einstein, Timothy Ferris, and Stephen Hawking, have worked hard to disassociate our minds from our current understanding of distance and time. Consider, for example, the following analogy.

Imagine yourself as an ant, standing on the one end of a rubber floor mat. To get to the other end, there's only one thing to do, right? You walk the surface of the mat until you get to the other end. You, the ant, are trapped in a two-dimensional world, in which "up" and "down" do not exist.

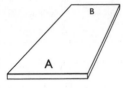

Now suppose that rubber floor mat was bent into a U-shape. As an ant, with no awareness of the third dimension, you would still be forced to walk the length of the mat, unaware that a simple leap from point A to point B would be much faster and more efficient. That's what Ferris and others feel is the secret to space travel: rather than crossing the horizontal distance, we must learn to see our galactic neighborhood in a different dimension, in which the shortcuts may be right under our collective nose.

Back here on Earth, the rubber floor mat analogy is an invitation for you to start bending the status quo in your professional and personal lives. So much of what we do is performed in an inefficient manner because "that's how we've always done it." We absorb the corporate culture around us and it becomes part of us. If meetings are a major source of time wastage (as many people say they are), then change how they're run. If customers or colleagues expect you to work on three things at once, then change their understanding and expectations of you. Break free of the two-dimensional standard and look for new avenues of positive achievement. The following are some examples.

Mail and E-Mail

Each day, information floods your office. Some is crucial, some is interesting, and much is unnecessary. It lands on your desk and it streams into your computer's e-mail folders. Numbering from dozens to hundreds of pieces of mail per day, it can soon overwhelm even the most diligent and organized among us.

The best way to avoid these piles of information is to never let them come to rest. Every letter, e-mail, and memo should find a home almost immediately upon arrival. An empty inbox reduces stress and allows for focus, consistency, and efficiency. It also eliminates one source of distraction and procrastination. Sure, it's difficult, but it's a habit you need to develop if you want to get any work done.

Incoming Mail
Avoid the temptation to read e-mail the moment it comes in.
Resisting is difficult for many people, since the "New Mail" alert pops up on the computer screen and provokes curiosity, making us think: "It could be important. Who could it be from? Maybe I should just take a quick look." But rushing to process every incoming piece of mail the moment it arrives is a key symptom of answerholism, since it fractures your day into smaller, unworkable parts. Instead, schedule your day to include message-returning periods. Maybe you'll need two, three, or four of them per day, but they will allow you to separate and concentrate the effort involved in reading and

responding to mail, while leaving larger blocks of time available for Keystone Period work, meetings, travel, and lunch — true optimization.

Assess each piece of mail quickly. With e-mail, this means scanning the subject line, not reading the entire document. With regular mail, it's easy to distinguish important-looking mail from junk mail, but it may be less simple to differentiate an important memo from a less-important one. This is where speed-reading and concentration really pay off.

Separate the high-priority items. List the items that must be acted upon immediately — or by the end of the day — on your calendar so that they stand out. Assign yourself a block of undisturbed time later in the day to deal with them. If they're that important, then they deserve such a block of time during your workday as a part of, not in addition to, your full complement of work hours. Identify and schedule medium-priority messages accordingly, throw the junk into the wastebasket immediately, and save trade magazines and periodicals for reading later. This technique of sorting and separating prevents your inbox from becoming a storage bin. Don't let mail hang around; otherwise, it may plant roots.

Work toward establishing a policy in your workplace. Many time management principles work much better when adopted by several people rather than just one. E-mail is a case in point. It would be worth your while to propose an e-mail policy that helps cut down on volume. Since e-mail is so easy to create and distribute, a lot of it gets passed around unedited, not polished or not really ready to be sent. Most of us have to waste time reading mail on which we are a courtesy copy (CC) recipient, rather than the addressee. Is this useful? Not if we have to spend ten minutes reading the entire thing just to see if there is anything important or relevant to us. This problem can be so great that some companies have even gone so far as to hire people to return other people's e-mail!

In the interest of proactive time management for all staff, not to mention reduced strain on the mail servers (an economic incentive!), it may be worthwhile to propose the following:

- that "high priority" red flags be used only for high priorities and in rare circumstances
- that the use of CC lists be eliminated, and that senders of e-mail should decide or be guided on how to keep the "To:" recipient list under control
- that executive summaries be included at the beginning of overly long e-mail documents and attachments
- that e-mail "Subject" lines clearly summarize the message
- that emphasis be placed on brevity and clarity, with most e-mails restricted to one screen in length

Master the art of reading fast. Read the Subject line, the first line of each paragraph, and the closing paragraph. With e-mail, as with other printed material, speed-reading is not only a useful technique; it's a survival technique!

Use the most time-efficient response method. Just because a message was sent to you by e-mail doesn't mean it has to be returned the same way. If it is quicker to leave a 15-second voice-mail message to the sender, then do that. If it is quicker to hit the "Reply" button and send your message that way, then do that. If it is quicker and clearer to wait until you meet that person face to face, then, by all means, do that. The trick is to take the focus away from the actual communication tools and put the focus back onto the message itself. What is the most efficient method of communicating with someone? The one that gets your message across without delay and without waste.

Return unreadable mail. If an e-mail arrives with an attachment that you can't open, or one that is unexpected, it is at best a waste of your time trying to open it, and at worst, if the attachment is a virus, a waste of many people's time trying to combat it. Call the sender and ask for clarification, confirmation, or a second copy.

Outgoing Mail

When it comes time to write letters, whether on paper or on a computer, keep the following in mind:

- Keep the subject line short and relevant. The subject line should summarize the letter in ten words or less.
- Keep the letter to one screen, or page, in length.
- Use bullet points rather than complete sentences.
- Never retype. If you or somebody else has already entered information, it should never have to be entered again. Use the copy and paste features of your word-processing and e-mail programs to place pre-written text into the body of your letter or send attachments.
- When sending attachments in e-mail, describe the attachment, including its name and which version of software it was saved in — and make sure it's virus-free before sending.
- In the body of the letter, indicate whether a response is necessary.

The Phone

The phone has always been a time management challenge. There was a time when voice mail and call display did not exist, and the black ringing phone had to be answered. Now, of course, that is not the case, and you are better off — from an efficiency and

achievement point of view —
not answering your phone. Yet
old habits die hard, and worse,
they're passed on to younger
generations.

Every call that comes in is an

Want to Travel Back in Time?

For an entertaining glimpse of what office
life used to be like, check out the movies
The Apartment (1960), starring Jack
Lemmon, and *Tin Men* (1987), starring
Richard Dreyfuss and Danny DeVito.

intrusion on your time. It's not just the duration of the call that is
intrusive, but the time needed for the follow-through, as well as
the time spent catching up mentally to the level of concentration
you enjoyed before the call.

So why, then, do we feel we must answer the phone?

A sense of achievement. You may feel that if you don't answer
the phone, things won't get done, business won't happen, connections won't be made. But not answering a call *at this
moment* is not the same as not answering it at all. There are
some occasions when live contact is essential, but much of
the time voice mail, like e-mail, can facilitate effective communication and time management by allowing for a concise,
no-nonsense transfer of information.

Fear of offending. You worry that not answering may send a
negative signal to the caller. In fact, we are all busy people,
and most people today are comfortable leaving voice mail.
Clear outgoing messages that ask for detailed messages or that
outline your scheduled times of availability, backed up by a
diligent routine of prompt call-returning, will soon "train"
your people that you are more accessible than ever, and
remind them that they remain important to you.

The desire to keep informed. There is a very real desire to be
kept "in the loop," or conversely a real fear of being left "out
of the loop" — so much so that some people take their cell

phones and pagers with them on vacation! A vacation isn't a vacation if you allow your work to follow you there. My main suggestion is to leave the work at home, and use your cell phones for family use and personal security only. Let the cell phone itself be a reminder of what your vacation stands for — after all, when its batteries run down, you have no choice but to give them time to recharge. Shouldn't you do yourself the same favor? If you absolutely have to stay in touch, I defer to the previous principle of scheduling distinct times throughout the day to check voice mail and e-mail. Allow them to occur between blocks of fun and relaxation. The key is to place the control over incoming messages back into your hands.

Ego. Some people need to answer each call because they feel they are too important to miss it. But there is a difference between needing to answer the phone and needing to receive information. This is the telephone equivalent of the open-door policy. Availability and accessibility can be maintained, and communication and learning can be upheld, without sacrificing efficiency, focus, and achievement.

The pleasure of socializing. Sometimes it's simply nice to talk. It proves a refreshing distraction, a period of leisure. If it feels good to talk, and if you need a few minutes' mental break, then do it, of course. But stay aware that the minutes are passing. The value of the time spent on the phone, in terms of productivity and efficiency, must always be considered.

Procrastination. Answering the phone can also serve as a handy excuse for putting off other work. When a task is difficult, unpleasant, or boring, almost anything else will appear far more attractive and important. When you reach to take or make a call, ask yourself: "Is this call directly in line with what

I'm doing now? Is it important enough?" Furthermore, is this call part of the critical path (see Chapter 4) necessary to complete this task? Or can this call be dealt with later?

A ringing phone carries with it certain presumptions of legitimacy and urgency. We are conditioned to believe that every call that comes in is important — more important than the work we are currently doing. But what if you were in a meeting or stuck in an elevator or in the dentist's chair when the call came in? Well, it would simply have to go into voice mail — there would be no choice. The call is still "important," but we're just not there to answer it.

You need to decide how important the phone is for you. For many people, the phone is useful as a messaging device. We leave voice-mail messages and expect to hear back within a reasonable turnaround time. We don't expect to get a live person on the other end, and it can be quite surprising when we do. The efficient time manager capitalizes on this by using the phone as a gatekeeper, a time management tool. Here are some ways to make wiser use of your phone:

- **Take advantage of call display.** When the phone rings, observe who is calling and use your judgment. Answer only the highest priority calls — those whose importance outweighs the importance of the work in front of you — and leave the rest for your message-returning period. If you don't have call display, get it. Call display is an essential business survival tool.

- **Let people know when you'll be calling back.** Change your outgoing voice mail greeting daily, and leave clear instructions as to when you will be returning calls. Something like:

You've reached Pat Smith of ABC Company for Tuesday the 16th. I'm currently in a meeting, but will be returning calls between 11:00 and noon, and again between 2:30 and 3:30 this afternoon. Please leave a detailed voice message and I will return your call at one of those times. If another time would be more convenient for you, please leave that time along with your message and I will do my best to connect with you then. Thank you.

The "meeting" this greeting refers to may be your Keystone Period. And yes, that is a meeting. This is another example of the deflect-and-save-face technique, and is the telephone equivalent of posting visiting hours outside your door. A customized voice-mail message lets people know they have reached you, and that they will indeed soon be receiving your undivided attention.

Front-Line Staff

If your job is based on answering every call before the third ring, then the telephone is your top priority, and this will impact the way you structure your day. A distinct message-returning period is not for you. It is still advisable to schedule a Keystone Period into each day, but it must be longer to accommodate the constraints of the incoming phone calls that are guaranteed to happen. You can still identify your number-one priority and assign it to your Keystone Period, but that period may have to be three hours or more in length to account for the distractions.

Making Phone Calls

When you make a call, you have the opportunity to practice time management in two directions: for you and for the recipient of the call. Here's how to go about it.

Make sure every call means something. If you reach another person's voice mail, be prepared to leave a message. Make a point. Be substantive. Prepare a point-form list of discussion items before calling, and use this as the agenda for your "telephone meeting," even if you are simply leaving a message. Address each point clearly and concisely before moving onto the next point, and be sure to leave your name, company name, and phone number at the start and the end of your message, pronouncing them clearly, especially if this is your first time communicating with a particular party.

Be conscious of small talk. Chatting can swallow up large amounts of your day. If you and the person you are calling are in need of an icebreaker or a brief mental break, then the value of small talk rises considerably. But often the reverse is true. Remember, even if you feel like small talk, the other person may not.

Have all relevant documents close at hand. If you are referring to a file, a letter, or a Web page, make sure it is within reach before making the call.

Take notes about the phone call during the call or immediately after. Make sure those notes are dated and filed in the appropriate file. Remember, this is part of the follow-through process, and helps make sure nothing falls between the cracks.

Time your calls. You'll be surprised at just how much time they take, especially when you consider that many calls can be dealt with in one-third of their current time. Stop and think for a moment. What is the average length of the phone calls you make? Five minutes? If you make 40 calls a week, that's three hours and 20 minutes spent on the phone. If you could, by using the techniques above, cut that time to a third, you would need to spend one hour and a few minutes each week in total on the phone, which returns to you two and a quarter hours of productive time. That's called refinement, and that's what the two-pound bucket is all about.

Receiving Phone Calls

When it comes time to play back the calls on your voice mail, or even when taking the occasional top-priority live call, make sure to enter the details in a call log. The design of this call log is up to you. You could use a simple word-processed document saved to your hard drive and made easily accessible via a shortcut on the desktop. It could be integrated with your calendar and address software, or it could be handwritten. The benefits of using a central call log are numerous:

- You can write down the time, caller, and message while listening to the message playback.
- All of your calls for an entire year or more — or all of the calls for a specific project — can be stored on one document and safely backed up. Doing this will remove the risk of misplacing phone numbers written on slips of paper.
- If you choose to use a word-processed file, you can use the "Find" feature of your word-processing software to quickly locate messages from days past.
- You can copy and paste messages from the central call log into the files of individual contacts.
- You can use the highlighter, bold, or any other feature of your word-processing software to emphasize action items (e.g., calls that must be returned, as opposed to calls that just give you information).
- E-mail and Web-page addresses entered into the central call log become active hyperlinks, allowing immediate access

to a pre-addressed e-mail letter or an Internet/intranet
Web page.

- The central call log can be reviewed once a week as you take
  your Bird's-Eye View (see Chapter 6), to ensure that no
  messages were missed, and that all calls and callers are
  satisfactorily accounted for.

Process each call actively, and deal with it in one of the following ways:

- **Handle:** If it can legitimately be called top priority and
  urgent, then get it done now. Otherwise,
- **Postpone:** Schedule the call for a more appropriate time —
  your message-returning period.
- **Refer:** Pass those calls/messages that can be dealt with by
  someone else.

If your return calls require you to leave voice-mail messages,
refer to the principles mentioned above, about making sure every
call means something. Once a call has been processed, remember
to follow through on the activity by scheduling any follow-ups
and then discarding the voice mail.

Telephone Tag

When your situation precludes using voice mail as a substitute
for live communication, telephone tag becomes a frustration.
Trying to get in touch with someone who is hard to reach can be
very frustrating. I suggest you set up an appointed time at which
you will connect. Leave a voice-mail message for your elusive
quarry that gives three times during which you guarantee to be
available and waiting. The message could go along these lines:

Pat, it's Steve. We've been playing telephone tag for a couple of days now, and I really think we should chat. I will be available between 2:00 and 2:30 on Wednesday, 4:00 and 6:00 on Thursday, and 9:00 and 10:00 on Friday. Let's set a date to talk. Whichever date is good for you, make sure to call me on my private cell number, 555-1234, so that it gets right through to me.

Please leave me a message today letting me know which one of these times is good for you, and I'll set the appointment.

That's how it works. Set an appointment to meet on the phone just as you would to meet in person. Schedule it accordingly, and respect its sanctity. Make sure you are there to receive the call at the given time and take no other calls. By keeping your appointments in this fashion, your reputation as a reliable, accessible professional will flourish, even while you administer your time on your own terms.

Meetings

Meetings are considered by many to be the single biggest time wasters in a workday. There are too many meetings — meetings with unclear agendas, meetings that go on for too long, and meetings that conclude with vague ideas and unresolved issues.

Why, then, do we have meetings? To coordinate action or exchange information, to motivate a team, to discuss problems, to make a decision. Do they always achieve these goals? Sometimes. Do they achieve them in the shortest time possible? Not often.

To make meetings run like clockwork, all you need are a few guiding principles, starting with an assessment of whether the meeting is really needed in the first place. The next time a meeting is called at which your presence is required, or if you are in charge of planning the next meeting, ask yourself first, "Is the meeting necessary?" Many meetings are called simply out of habit, which adversely affects the schedules and productivity of the people involved, as well as their support staff and the other people with whom attendees could be meeting instead. Could the same information be delivered via a telephone conference, a videoconference, or a simple e-mail?

Here is your opportunity to bend the status quo, to break free of the corporate tradition of having meetings for everything — meetings that everyone is expected to attend. Meetings should instead be seen as valuable summits of a communications hierarchy, in which expensive and busy people spend their valuable time efficiently exchanging clear ideas in the name of moving forward. Does that sound a little far-fetched? The following paragraphs give you a few suggestions for making meetings work without sucking all the time out of the day.

Prepare an agenda and plan the time allotted for each item. Sounds pretty straightforward, but lots of meetings start with only a general idea of what to cover. Others start with an agenda, but fail to set the amount of time allowed for each item. Both of these result in unbalanced and misused time. If you are the chairperson, your responsibility is to think through the meeting well before it happens. Identify the topics to be covered and list them. Be realistic as to time — there are only so many things that can be talked about in a given time block.

For example, a one-hour meeting will probably only have time for two or three items and might look like the one on the next page.

The *call to order* is an official opening of the meeting. If you have access to a gavel, then use it. Judges and auctioneers do so for a reason. The sound is audible, unmistakable, and carries great authority. The *meeting officials* are the chairperson, who officially hosts the meeting, the timekeeper, the arbiter, and the minute-taker, all of whom are described in more detail below.

Agenda
Tuesday the 5th, 10:00–11:00

10:00	Call to order, introduction of meeting officials, housekeeping
10:05	Item 1 (15 minutes)
10:20	Item 2 (15 minutes)
10:35	Item 3 (15 minutes)
10:50	Summary, action items (5 minutes)
10:55	Closing
11:00	Adjournment

As chairperson, part of your role is to decide not only what will be talked about during the meeting, but how this information will be presented. Will you entertain questions as events unfold, or save them all until the end? Will you allow debate? Is the goal of the meeting to share ideas across the table, or to deliver a pre-packaged collection of facts? Decide, and then mention these points during the opening of the meeting. Also make sure that these rules are in the agenda.

Circulate the agenda in advance — two or three days in advance, if possible. Doing this has two benefits. First, it allows people to come to the meeting already prepared to discuss the items, rather than facing them for the first time once the

Pop Quiz: Agendas

If you are the chair of the next meeting, and you estimate that each agenda item will be allowed 15 minutes, how many agenda items could you schedule in an hour?

The answer is not four, but three. Get into the habit of recognizing that a meeting consists of more than the cut-and-dried agenda items. Opening and closing remarks, questions, housekeeping announcements – these all need time.

Keep this quiz in mind, and your meetings will stand a better chance of starting and ending on time.

meeting gets underway. Second, it is a contract, or a set of ground rules, as to what the meeting will cover — and perhaps more importantly, what it will *not* cover. The agenda need not be circulated for approval or modification, but serves merely as advance notice of the topics to be discussed, and fair warning for all attendees to arrive prepared.

Start on time. Doing this is extremely important. Starting on time shows respect for people who are punctual and exemplifies leadership on your part. It also serves as a reminder to those who are habitually late that it is they who must adapt, not the rest of the group. Make a point of mentioning the time as you begin, so as to demonstrate your willingness to get underway on time, as promised. An on-time start sets a positive note, and adds credence to the promise that the meeting will also end on time. If some of the attendees are guests, the on-time start also reflects extremely well on the company as a whole. Being polite and waiting for someone who is late doesn't carry as much currency as an efficient, punctual kick-off.

YES, BUT... What if it is the president or CEO who is late? That person probably has a good excuse for being late, but it is still no excuse for delaying the meeting. If the not-yet-arrived CEO is scheduled to deliver the opening speech, use the time for other agenda items. After all, a group of people physically together is a tremendous and rare opportunity to communicate. If the CEO is merely to be in attendance, and his or her participation is not necessary to get the meeting underway, then get started. People may ultimately have good excuses for not arriving on time, but there is no excuse for not starting on time.

Consider the dollar value of all those people sitting around a boardroom table, biding their time waiting for the meeting to start — 9:05, 9:10, 9:15 . . . If you have ten people in attendance, all waiting for the 11th and 12th to appear, take a moment to calculate your hourly rate (even if you're on salary you can do this), then multiply by 12. That quickly becomes a lot of money per minute sitting around the table. Now double it, to take into account the other things that your attendees are not doing but *could* be doing if they were back at their desks. Soon you'll arrive at an amount equivalent to the loss of a computer, or front-end damage to the company car. These are tangible amounts of money being lost due to meetings not starting on time.

Toastmasters

If you're interested in learning about and practicing the art of speaking at – and running – meetings, consider visiting your local Toastmasters chapter. Founded in 1924, Toastmasters provides a supportive environment to practice and develop speaking and leadership skills.

To find a chapter near you, visit www.toastmasters.org.

Call the meeting to order and announce the agenda, including scheduled break times. Inform attendees when refreshments will be arriving, and ask them to set their cell phones to "silent."

Stick to the agenda and to the times allotted for each item. As chairperson of the meeting, be clear that speakers have a fixed number of minutes to make their point. Demonstrate this by wrapping up each agenda item on time. The only exception to this rule is if you are on such a roll with a particular topic that wrapping up would be counterproductive, but even then, make mention of the time and your desire to modify the agenda before continuing. Keep to the time limits, and use diplomatic but firm instructions if speakers are running overtime or drifting off topic. A meeting that is kept to an agenda and within time limits is not a demonstration of demagoguery or power-madness. In fact, it's quite the reverse. It's a demonstration of the respect you hold for the time and the priorities of the attendees.

Assign a timekeeper. This person will keep a close eye on the time allotted for each agenda item, will use hand signals to count down the minutes available to a speaker, and will ensure time limits are respected by alerting the group with the gavel, or even simply by tapping a pen against a glass. By assigning a timekeeper at the beginning of the meeting, in front of the meeting atten-dees, you are bestowing to this person the authority to keep time and to act as a neutral official of the meeting. This practice goes a long way in saving face when a participant gets "carried away" and needs to be reminded when his or her time is up.

Assign a minute-taker. This person takes notes. The notes need not be a verbatim transcript, but should cover

- the key points raised,
- who raised them, and
- what is to be done next and by whom.

The minutes must be able to answer these three points for each agenda item, and if the minute-taker is not clear on any one of them, he or she has the right and obligation to ask and clarify before the meeting adjourns. If the minute-taker is comfortable using a laptop computer during the meeting, then minutes will almost prepare themselves. Minutes should also include the name, phone number/extension, and e-mail address of the chair-person and the minute-taker in case the need for questions and clarifications arises.

Assign an arbiter. This person will be given the authority to step in and referee if discussions get heated or off-topic. By assigning this role to someone other than you, both the chair-person (you) and the arbiter will achieve more recognition and endorsement from the attendees. It is better that the arbiter be someone other than the timekeeper or the minute-taker, as they will already have enough to do.

Have a side-sheet available for non-agenda items, or schedule time for them at the end of the meeting. Meetings always bring forth other points and ideas, but if they're not relevant to the agenda, they should be recognized and then scheduled for later. Some meeting managers plan an extra 15 minutes at the end of a meeting to discuss these extra items. Others add the new items to the agenda for the next meeting. Don't let off-topic discussions take over the current meeting if you wish to achieve your current meeting's stated goals. Here, then, is the revised agenda:

Agenda
Tuesday the 5th, 10:00–11:15

10:00	Call to order, introduction of meeting officials, housekeeping
10:05	Item 1 (15 minutes)
10:20	Item 2 (15 minutes)
10:35	Item 3 (15 minutes)
10:50	Off-agenda items (10 minutes)
11:00	Summary, action items (10 minutes)
11:10	Closing
11:15	Meeting adjourned

– Minutes will be distributed within 24 hours.

Invite the right people. Ensure that everyone who is to attend the meeting has something to contribute, rather than simply inviting "everyone on the list." By making sure that only those who need to be at the meeting are invited, you are demonstrating respect for the busy schedules of both the invitees and the non-invitees. Careful meeting planning also exemplifies key leadership abilities.

Dismiss participants when they are no longer needed. If people have better things to do with their time, let them go after the agenda items most relevant to them are complete. Meetings should be about productivity, not time. The remaining attendees will immediately and unconsciously refocus the energy of the room, allowing greater concentration on the next agenda item. Ensure that all attendees, including those who leave early, are on the list to receive the full minutes of the meeting.

Decide upon the next steps for each agenda item and make them known. Merely assuming that everyone knows the next step is never enough — this is a major source of confusion and delay in many organizations. Be sure that each participant leaves the room with a clear understanding of what is to follow for each agenda item. Make sure the minute-taker clearly understands the next step. Have him or her read back the next-step items from the minutes before the meeting adjourns.

End on time. Doing so demonstrates your respect for the busy schedules of your attendees, as well as your leadership and organizational skills. It is a fulfilment of the "contract" you distributed in the form of a pre-circulated agenda. It allows people to plan their days accurately around your meetings, knowing that a promised 11:15 end will indeed occur at 11:15. It is also a welcome relief for those who have attended more than their share of drawn-out gatherings.

Be a proactive chairperson. Demonstrate your leadership by employing time-efficient meeting tactics clearly, and making sure all group members know you are at the helm. Delegate the responsibilities of timekeeper, minute-taker, and arbiter. State your goals for this meeting and the meeting's end time clearly, right at the beginning. Allow enough time at the end of the meeting to briefly summarize the key points, achievements, and follow-ups for each agenda item. Thank all members for their participation, remind them to turn their phones back on, and end the meeting on an upbeat note. Make sure all attendees leave the meeting with a clear understanding of what was said and what is to happen next, and thank them for their time. Make a point of officially drawing the meeting to a close, rather than allowing people to simply shuffle out.

Prepare and circulate minutes of the meeting. This should occur no more than 24 hours after the meeting. Be sure to factor the time required to prepare and circulate the minutes as a scheduled activity, not just as a vague notion. Minutes are part of the meeting, or more precisely, part of the follow-through procedure of the meeting activity.

Back-to-Back Meetings

If you have any say in this at all, don't plan meetings back-to-back. Plan for breathing space between meetings. Allow yourself time to collect your thoughts, follow through on the activities of the previous meeting, and refresh yourself before the next meeting.

Use your between-meeting breathing space to breathe. Don't use it to take on additional tasks such as returning phone calls or running back to the office. This simply introduces new and irrelevant ideas and preoccupations at a time when you should be focusing on the meeting ahead, and it's a guarantee that you'll end up late.

The Healthy, Productive Meeting Room

A meeting room should be viewed and treated as an equal partner in the meeting. Its contribution to the meeting will be to help maintain energy levels and elicit proactive thought from all attendees. Wherever possible, meetings should be scheduled as much around the availability of the optimum room as around the availability of the participants. Look for a room with natural light, good air circulation, little white noise, and no meetings going on next door.

Many corporate meeting rooms already provide at least some of these features, but people tend to overlook their importance, opting merely for the first room available. When rooms with adequate climate and noise control do become available, they are not fully exploited because no one is aware of the importance of these elements of a successful meeting — or no one knows how to work the controls on the wall. Try using the following list of essential meeting room necessities when assessing your next location.

Lighting

Choose a room that is lit with incandescent light (bulbs) rather than fluorescent light. If your meeting room has both, turn off the fluorescent lights and bring the incandescents to a 75 percent lighting level. This light is easier on the eyes, allowing attendees to remain alert and avoid sleepiness from a room that is too dark, or eye fatigue and headaches from the incessant green-tinged flickering of fluorescent lighting. Also, if one end of the room will be used for delivering a presentation, ensure you have separate lighting controls that allow the presenter and the material to be adequately lit. Clearly mark the light switches, using masking tape if necessary, so that lights can be controlled smoothly and correctly, not only by you but also by anyone else around the table.

The human metabolism craves natural light. Any time you can book a boardroom with a window, do it. Even when the blinds have to be drawn for a presentation, the presence of natural light so close by provides energy and stamina for the attendees. Whenever possible, keep the blinds open to allow the natural light to flood the room.

Churches and Temples: Practical Designs for Regular Meetings

For centuries, churches and temples have stood as outstanding examples of the power of effective meeting spaces. Their architecture is intended to inspire the appropriate feelings from their congregations. The air is scented and the lights are warm and colorful, all to provide an enhanced sensory experience.

Perhaps most importantly, the entrances are always at the end farthest from the altar to accommodate latecomers without distraction.

Air circulation

Along with light, good air helps keep our metabolic systems charged and invigorated. Meetings that go on for more than 20 minutes are in great danger of losing the attention of attendees if good air is not available. Your room should first and foremost have good air delivery. This means choosing a room that has either windows that open (good luck!) or a manually controlled air conditioning/fan system. In my opinion, meetings should never be held in basement rooms or small, windowless offices.

Locate the manual temperature control and clearly mark it with masking tape. Set the temperature of the room to about 68°F (20°C), which is cool without being cold, but make sure to ask how people are feeling during the meeting. If the temperature needs to be raised or lowered, do so. On the whole, it's better to have a room a little on the cool side than overly warm. If meetings go on for hours, or if the room is booked for back-to-back meetings throughout the day, it is essential that the circulation system do its job in replacing stale air regularly and completely. Also consider using a humidifier or ionizer to help maintain air quality.

Noise

Noise distracts. A meeting is supposed to be an exercise in communication and education. Too much noise will distract attendees from your message. A healthy meeting room should have little or no white noise: the hiss that comes from heating/air systems, projection systems, overhead projectors, and computers. When you assess a meeting room, stand perfectly still and listen for white noise. Check the sound level when the air circulation fan is on. Check the "distraction factor" when the air circulation system shuts off or turns on. Will this noise be too much of a disturbance, or can you work around it?

Will there be noise from other meeting rooms? If two meeting rooms are separated by a removable wall and the speaker in the adjoining meeting has a powerful voice, or there is laughter, applause, or the sound of movement, these can't fail to be a distraction that proves counterproductive to your meeting. Check with the person who books meeting rooms and look for one that is as isolated as possible. Will there be noise from traffic outside, or construction/renovation within the building? Again, find out about these possibilities from the appropriate sources before booking your room.

Phones

Ask that all cell phones be set on "silent," so that calls can still get through, and people can excuse themselves to take the call if they must, without disturbing the other attendees. People should really let their voice mail take the calls during meetings. However, if they insist on bringing their cell phones in, you can insist on having the phones muzzled. The same rule should be applied to the meeting-room phone itself. Instruct the switchboard to allow only top-priority calls through.

Decor

I have attended some meetings where the room says, "Here is where office furniture comes to die." Such a room has boxes, old computers, and old broken chairs stacked in the corners and a picture, whose frame was broken in an office move, still sitting on the floor with shards of glass around it.

I have also been to meetings in the boardrooms of some very successful companies, where mahogany and leather furnishings are in perfect harmony, video projector systems descend from hidden compartments in the ceiling, natural light floods the room, sound levels are perfect, and original artwork hangs on the walls.

The difference in the productivity potential of the meetings held in these two types of rooms is enormous. Energy, attention, and constructive, creative thought can be magnified by the physical attributes of the meeting place. Not everyone has the luxury of a well-appointed, high-tech boardroom, but we all have the ability to assess our resources and plan accordingly. The efficient use of the time of everyone invited to the meeting is at stake.

Seating

If you are convening in a boardroom, the obvious layout for seating your participants is around the boardroom table. However, if there is no central table, there are other layouts that will help heighten communication and productivity potential through "intimacy." If you have sectional tables, for example, rearrange them into a U-shape (see top diagram on page 69). If there are no tables at all, arrange the chairs into a "V" formation (see bottom diagram on page 69).

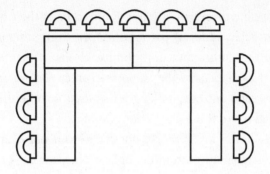

U-shape

V formation

Both of these layouts allow clear sightlines for all participants, along with an atmosphere more conducive to discussion, since all attendees can see each other.

If possible, structure your meeting room so that the door is at the "back" of the room, as far as possible from the presenter. This helps minimize the distraction caused by latecomers.

Seating is crucial to the time-efficient running of a meeting not only in terms of layout, but also in terms of the seats themselves. Since most people spend much of their meeting time sitting down, comfortable chairs are a must. Why is this important to time management? Because people who are uncomfortable or in pain are not going to be at their best. This results in delay, reduced participation, or even absenteeism. If you have the choice and opportunity, choose a meeting room with comfortable chairs that support correct posture and alignment. Try each one out, looking for squeaks or other distracting noises, and move those chairs out of range.

Sounds like a lot of work, doesn't it? But preparations like these are similar to putting enough gas in your car before you need it, or measuring a doorway before you buy furniture. They are investments in proactive time management that will pay off in more productive time-efficient meetings: meetings in which distractions are held to a minimum, energy is kept high, and ideas are clearly understood and thoroughly acted upon.

Refreshments

They're more than just welcome at meetings — they're essential. Coffee and tea are standard, but to ensure your participants remain refreshed and hydrated, keep plenty of water on hand. Ask for cold water, of course, but if you can, leave the ice cubes out. They are too distracting when poured into a glass. Food is also useful. Remember, however, that the "fun" foods, such as donuts and pastries, are full of empty calories that do nothing to provide stamina for the rest of the meeting, and will generate sluggishness as soon as the sugar has burned off. Consider low-fat muffins and fresh fruit, high-water-content vegetables such as carrots, celery, and cauliflower, and small sandwiches if a real lunch needs to be served. Avoid foods high in fat, such as pizza, and those that are high in carbohydrates or starch, such as pasta salad and potatoes. They will make everyone sluggish, especially as the afternoon wears on. For more on the importance of nutrition and food as a time management tool, see the section on food in Chapter 7.

Breaks

If your meeting is scheduled to last 90 minutes or more, then be absolutely sure to schedule a break. Though this threatens at first glance to lengthen the meeting, it actually helps to shorten it by providing an environment of heightened productivity in less time. Humans need breaks, and 90 minutes of concentration is about the limit people can endure.

Technology

Many meetings use technology to assist in the presentation of ideas. Nothing ruins the momentum and the time-efficient, positive flow of a presentation like "technical problems."

If you are planning to use an overhead projector, pre-book and reserve the projector and screen. Have a spare bulb for the overhead projector, and ensure both projector and screen are set up and ready before the attendees file in. Have your acetates ready, framed, and in the right order.

If you are planning to use a computer in conjunction with a data projector, ensure that the presentation is saved on the computer and that you can find the file. Rehearse the presentation, including how to move back one slide, how to move to any slide in the presentation, and how to end the show with a closing slide. Ensure the data projector is available and that it is compatible with your system. Have acetate or other hard-copy backup in case of projector failure. Schedule time for advance setup. Ensure that the window blinds provide adequate darkness.

A Low-Cost Trip Hazard and Lawsuit Shield

Cables are a constant hazard when giving presentations. If you have to lay extension cords across an area of floor where people will be walking, take a piece of flip-chart paper and roll it around the cables, forming a tube, then tape this tube closed. This keeps all the cables neat, and also provides a clear visual alert to their presence.

If you are planning a presentation that requires access to the Internet, make sure the data jack is clearly marked to avoid damage to the network or phone system. Get clear instructions in advance on how to connect. Have the name and phone number of a technician on call, and most importantly, have an off-line copy of your presentation, either in hard copy or on your computer, in case an Internet connection cannot be made.

In all situations in which technology plays a central role in a presentation, my rule is a simple one: make sure you can complete the presentation without using the technology at all. Many meetings and presentations have had to limp to an early conclusion due to user inexperience or technology failure. This situation is not only embarrassing, it also wastes time for all involved. In adhering to the "pay me now or pay me later" rule (see Chapter 4), take the time to ensure you can deliver the entire presentation without using electronic technologies. This may require the creation of paper handouts and/or being sufficiently familiar with the content to be able to ad lib and create illustrations on a flip chart or whiteboard. Sure, they may not be as slick as your original show, but if they get the job done, then they just might save the day.

One additional point: Having the "tech-free" version of your presentation accessible is a major stress reliever. First, it eliminates the worry of "What happens if something goes wrong?" and, more importantly, if something *does* go wrong, you will be able to switch effortlessly to your tech-free version and continue being your best, without succumbing to panic or embarrassment. That is the essence of Cool Time (see Chapter 8).

Personal Habits

A reminder now that this chapter focuses on bending the status quo: changing habits and procedures in your corporate life in the interest of efficient time management. There are likely a few personal habits or methods of doing things that you could change, personality aspects that hold you back from true satisfaction with the way you spend your time. Therefore, this next section deals with some of the most common impediments to personal progress.

Procrastination

When it comes down to getting tasks done, there will always be at least one that you just don't want to do. It may hold the least appeal to you, it may be the least rewarding, or it may involve confrontation, unpleasant tasks, or drudgery. It also makes every other task on your list look instantly more appealing.

Procrastination is about putting off something that is obviously important, that could or should be done now, but that you just don't want to do. Procrastination puts negative feelings into your heart and mind. The longer you procrastinate, the longer you live with a shadow of guilt, dread, and the pang of the inevitable. The main problem with procrastination is the persistent awareness of the task that remains unstarted. It's hard to enjoy your leisure time with such an albatross around your neck. Procrastination extends the life of that task, making it longer than it truly deserves to be. A task delayed by 14 days suddenly becomes a 14-day-long task, which is a lot of time to spend feeling bad.

The only way to deal with procrastination is to get the task done, as soon as it is both possible and proper. Using your I-Beam Review and priority chart (see Chapter 4), step back and assess this task in relation to the others. Is it important and urgent, or important and not urgent? Should the task be done now, even though you don't want to do it, or can it be legitimately scheduled for a later time? Plan a time for the performance of the task in accordance with your other priorities.

What about delegation? Could or should this task be assigned to somebody else who has the time, skills, or experience to take it off your hands? Don't let the gravity of the task cloud your judgment when other resources may be close at hand.

If the chore seems overly large and its sheer size is one of the factors contributing to your procrastination, break it down into subtasks. Not only does this help to plan and direct the task to a successful conclusion, but the positive feeling of achievement gained from completing each subtask will help fuel your motivation and help you get on with the rest.

Create a timeline on paper. Get a sense of timing and priority by lining up the component tasks backwards from the due date to the latest possible start date (this is called the "critical path," and is discussed in more detail in Chapter 4). The timeline helps establish perspective, the Bird's-Eye View. It clearly defines each step, making each task easier to take on. Also, by getting the plan down on paper, the start and end points turn into tangible, visible elements, which allows your mind to truly buy in to the reality of completing the task. Be sure to add some "lag time" — extra hours or days between tasks, as appropriate — so as to give yourself some room for rest, redoing, or other unrelated tasks.

Taxes: Homework for Grownups

Just as spring arrives, with its warmer weather and its promise of good days to come, so, too, does the specter of income tax. Few adults relish the thought of doing taxes — it's a sacrifice of weekend or evening time.

What's the best way to get through it? Focus on that moment when they're all completed, when you slip the forms in the mailbox and have done with them.

Picture in your mind that feeling of liberation, of victory. Think of all those weekends and evenings now stretching out before you. Bribe yourself with the awareness of how good it will feel when you're done.

Do it. Get it over with. Then enjoy your summer.

Focus on the Finish

Envision the task as already completed. Picture, in your mind, the end result of the chore and the feeling it gives you to see it finished. Buy in to its existence so that its completed state becomes real in your imagination. Before every competition, professional athletes see themselves at the finish line, victorious. They make it real. By picturing your unpleasant task in its completed state, you focus your mind, your energies, and your determination.

Plan the Next Step

Picture what happens next. Envision the follow-through. This helps make the task easier by granting you perspective of what lies ahead. For example, if you were responsible for letting an employee go as part of your company's downsizing, such a task might seem overwhelmingly difficult and unpleasant for you, especially when you consider that person's family, responsibilities, personality, and contributions to the company so far. But if this is an inevitable action, something that you must do now, is it not better to get through the actual termination process and move quickly toward healing? You can help that person get over the shock of termination, locate resources and counselors for the transition period, and set the person on his or her way. All tasks, even unpleasant ones, have other tasks and events that follow. Take a Bird's-Eye View of the situation and use your longer-range perception to provide incentive for dealing with the unpleasant task at hand.

Use a Reward System

Give yourself a reward for completing the undesirable task. Perhaps this means going home early, or buying yourself something, or moving on to a different task, one that you'd rather do. A reward makes for a powerful incentive to counter the forces of procrastination. Like icing on the cake, the reward seems doubly pleasurable since your conscience will be clear, and the weight of the onerous task will have been lifted from your shoulders.

Accept the Inevitable

Some things just have to get done. The sooner you take the bull by the horns, the sooner you can get past the unpleasant task and on to the things you prefer. Time spent procrastinating is not pleasurable time. It is hard time. Life is too short to allow hours or days to be spent under the cloud of looming guilt. The value, the pleasure, the release that is felt upon completion of an unpleasant task moves you back onto a healthy track of achievement and self-determination.

Working to the Last Minute

When you combine procrastination with a deadline, you very quickly arrive at the "last minute." Are you a last-minute person? Do you work on projects perilously close to the deadline? Do you do your holiday shopping during that last frantic week? Did you (or do you still) cram for exams or stay up late writing reports and essays? Do you promise yourself that next time you're going to get organized?

Leaving tasks to the last minute guarantees sub-par performance, fatigue, and stress. To make matters worse, this occasionally requires you to repeat the task due to errors, omissions, or other defects. Some people will say they work better under pressure, but in truth the only benefit derived from working to a deadline is a fatalistic self-justification, one that says, "Hey, I did the best I could. There was no more time. Leave me alone."

By leaving things to the last minute, you are backing yourself into an emotional corner in which the responsibility for top-notch performance is replaced by a higher priority: that of merely getting something — anything — done in time. We can look back at our school years as the breeding ground for this counterproductive technique, when papers and assignments would sit untouched for days or weeks, only to evolve into a crescendo

The Coast Guard Rule

The U.S. Coast Guard has a rule for fueling boats that epitomizes the type of thinking necessary for avoiding last-minute crunches: the top third of a tank is fuel for going out. The bottom third of the tank is fuel for coming back. The middle third is for surprises.

of harried activity, all-nighters, and requests for extensions.

The pressure to perform under such last-minute conditions creates stress, which affects the very areas of the mind required for creative, intelligent thought. Memory, logical reasoning, idea production, and decision-making ability will all be sacrificed as the innate fight-or-flight reflex activates in the face of a fast-looming threat. In short, last-minute labor is a guarantee that your work will not be its best.

Some people may already be aware that last-minute work is less-than-optimum work, yet they favor this technique because it eliminates any opportunity for proofing, review, or improvement — which, though desirable, may mean having to put more work in on a job that comes back for revision. To this, the efficient time manager must apply the "pay me now or pay me later" rule (see Chapter 4), which basically states that you either invest the effort up front to get it right the first time, or you spend time later fixing it. Either way, you'll be spending more time on the project than you'd hoped, so you might as well take a little longer, plan that extra time into your schedule, and do it right the first time.

The solution to the last-minute syndrome is found in back-planning and project management. Once you are notified of a task or project, don't get stuck into it immediately. Take some time to plan. Identify the project's key components. Start scheduling from the deadline backwards, taking into account all the other unrelated tasks you have to do. Don't let wishful thinking replace clear vision. If a project must get done, then it must get done properly. The effective time manager remembers to factor in adequate time for revisions, corrections, delivery, mistakes, delays, and modifications.

Breaking Tasks Up

Along with procrastination and working to the last minute, another personal time management faux pas comes from breaking tasks up rather than forging through to their completion. Each task should be seen as an indivisible component of action, to be started and completed within a fixed period. If a task is interrupted, the sum total of minutes it takes to complete the task, before and after the interruption, will be greater than if it is completed in one shot. Each time you return to an unfinished task, your mind and body need to regroup and rebuild momentum.

Obviously, work that takes three days to complete must be divided into tasks in order to guarantee progress. The idea here is once again to be conscious of the power of your activities within time. By taking a moment to plan and to subdivide activities into component tasks, aiming to complete one task at a time, you will achieve real progress.

Successful completion of tasks feels good. Crossing them off a list of to-do's feels good and will spur on even more good work. Conversely, if you leave a task unfinished, you leave with no sense of accomplishment, which weighs negatively on the psyche and invites delay, distraction, and procrastination.

If a project or assignment cannot be completed in one go, if it requires too many hours or resources and must be split up, then from a time management perspective you stand to gain more from doing some planning first. For example, if you have three hours to perform a piece of work and it's obvious by the end of the second hour that the work will not be completed by the end of hour three, it makes more sense to invest the last 15 minutes of hour three in planning the next steps than it does to just simply work to the absolute end of the hour.

Once again, this all comes down to project management, in which "planning" is the primary tool and "doing" is secondary.

Firefighting

Firefighting is the art of quickly resolving a crisis and making the best of the situation. There are some who pride themselves on being masters at putting out such "fires." Much like last-minute people, firefighters move from crisis to crisis, defusing panic situations and restoring order.

> **What a Fiasco!**
>
> *Fiasco* is a term used to describe a mess, a screw-up, the kind of thing you don't want to have happen again.
>
> It comes from the Italian word for "bottle." When the glassblowers of medieval Italy made a mistake and their beautiful, delicate glass sculpture collapsed while being blown, all they could do to cut their losses was to reshape the glass and sell their ruined work as a bottle, a *fiasco*.

They are addicted to the rush of a situation's urgency and to the fact that they alone can be the hero. But firefighting is not something to which the efficient time manager should aspire. Even real firefighters, those who work at fire stations, would prefer that people take precautions to avoid as many real disasters as possible.

It is better not to have a crisis at all. Firefighting may help to resolve an immediate problem, but it does so at a great price. It requires that you focus your resources and energies on a situation that shouldn't ever have been allowed to exist. It diverts you from the real priorities of the day, priorities that will now have to be put off, which in turn compounds your existing workload and builds a mountain of unstarted and unfinished work. Fighting fires also means using instant, hurried judgment, risking irrational, improper decisions and less-than-productive outcomes.

The solution to avoiding fires and firefighting is prevention, and the method is lifted from classic project management theory:

Plan everything thoroughly. Planning prevents crises. Plan your day, your week, your projects, and the availability of your resources. Doing this allows you to foresee possible problems and factor for contingencies. If crises do occur, your same project and day plans will act as a guide, helping to determine what tasks must be put aside in order to fight the fire and when they can be rescheduled.

Anticipate what might happen. Make plans to prevent the bad things from happening. Yes, it's extra effort, but it's central to project management and project success. It's the ounce of prevention versus the pound of cure.

Prepare and keep a crisis-management checklist. If crises do occur, it is safer to rely on established procedure than seat-of-the-pants thinking. Include procedures, contact names, and telephone numbers. Make sure that at least two people in the office are fully familiar with the list and their responsibilities.

Take advantage of lessons from the past by recording information on past projects, including their problems, mistakes, and crises. Factor their challenges and triumphs into your current project plan as well as your crisis checklist.

Plan for cushion periods. When performing your I-Beam Review (see Chapter 4), and also when planning your projects, make sure to give yourself a cushion. Calculate all your deadlines or end times and then add at least 20 percent more. More often than not, projects take more time to complete than initially expected. That is why experienced project managers build "slack time" into schedules, and "pad" estimated times to completion. They know that putting down on paper the expected time of completion in a perfect world, under perfect circumstances, is an invitation to grief and stress very soon thereafter.

Make no mistake! You will need extra time. Your estimates can be made intelligently from diaries of projects past, from the input of experienced team members, and from calculated planning. Build your cushion periods in at the start. These are legitimate parts of a project, and anyone who questions them is inexperienced in managing projects.

What If the Crisis Is Happening Now?

If you are in the midst of a crisis now, count to ten and avoid panic. There are rules to follow in a crisis situation:

Be aware of overreaction and try to avoid it. Crises do have solutions. They may require urgent phone calls, changes of plans, fast travel, and fast thinking, but crises can be resolved. What is crucial during a crisis situation is clear thinking and the avoidance of "alarm mindset." Don't fall prey to your first instinct. Take a moment to assess the situation and plan the most expedient and practical course of events to solve it.

Avoid the superhero syndrome. This is the feeling that everything must be done by you and you alone. It is commonly felt by people who are used to decision-making and fast action. However, more can be done through delegation and leadership than by becoming a single-person rescue squad. Take the time to assess your resources, assign tasks appropriately, and follow up with them to ensure nothing gets left behind.

Use checklists. If you have prepared a crisis checklist, be sure to use it. Make sure you know where it is. Make sure other people know where it is and how to use it, as the odds are always greatest that the person who best knows what to do in a particular crisis will be on vacation when it happens.

Ask yourself, "What would happen if I did nothing?" Some crises can be left to blow themselves out. Urgency and adrenaline sometimes make us do more than is actually necessary. Assess the nature of the crisis and consider whether your actions would solve or prolong the situation. Consider what the implications of this crisis will be a year from now. Take a Bird's-Eye View and put the problem into perspective (see Chapter 6).

Panic is contagious — don't let it infect you. When one person displays signs of panic, it becomes very easy for it to spread to everyone. Don't let panic and rash thinking cloud your judgment or that of others. Cool heads always prevail. Think before, think during, and think after.

Loss of Momentum and Inertia

Another place to change the status quo with regard to personal productivity techniques centers on what happens when creativity or ability grinds to a halt. You're under pressure to get your work done. You can hear the seconds ticking away, yet it's just not working right and with every passing moment the tension increases. What is the most time-efficient way of dealing with such inertia? *Do something else.* The human mind is a marvelous tool, but there are times when inspiration doesn't flow, even though you and your people really wish it would. In the corporate context where time is money and delay means stress, the longer the blockage lasts, the greater the pressure on everyone involved. Thus, it would seem that the last thing you should do is to "walk away" from the project and do something different.

But this is exactly what will help clear the logjam and rebuild momentum, especially if the "something else" is something mentally relaxing, such as a workout, a massage, or a walk outside. From a time management perspective, this step backward will become two steps forward, for a mind released is a mind freed of tensions.

When inertia strikes, don't fall prey to the panic of the moment. As it is with so many areas of life, there is much more to be gained from stepping back, slowing down, and relaxing.

Training Your Co-workers

Possibly one of the most difficult things about implementing a time management plan is getting it accepted by your colleagues, clients, and managers. Fear of rocking the boat or appearing "strange" dissuades us from putting efficient techniques into action. But this is what bending the status quo is all about: no longer looking along the two-dimensional plane of convention but jumping forth into a new dimension of ability and proactive thinking. If you are to chair your next meeting, then start applying some of the principles in the Meetings section, above. If you are not the chairperson, then ask the chairperson, "Where's the agenda?" "Who is the timekeeper?" "Who are you inviting?" If you are looking to get more out of your day, then start using a Keystone Period, and let your people know what it is, why it works, and when you'll be available. Shape your voice-mail and e-mail technique to ensure timely and efficient communication without sacrificing your precious working minutes.

Nothing succeeds like success in these matters. A client of mine recently pointed out a senior broker in his company who maintained one of the most profitable portfolios in the company's history. He came in at 10:00, worked for two hours without interruption, then took two hours for lunch, most of it at the local gym. Why did nobody dare bother him during his Keystone Period? His track record spoke for itself. His undisturbed Keystone Period made him the most profitable broker on the floor.

If you, too, start to implement some of these Cool Time techniques of time management, and start to record and demonstrate your increased abilities, energies, and achievements, these will serve as an impressive sales tool for introducing change throughout your department. Maintain communication with your colleagues and clients as you change your status quo. Let them know why you are doing these things and why they work. Consciously, actively, intelligently change how "things are done" for the better.

4

The I-Beam Review: Planning and Structure

If you gave me six hours to chop down a tree, I would spend four sharpening my axe.

— ABRAHAM LINCOLN

Planning is the secret to success in project management. A project that does not have a strong plan in place — a plan that anticipates problems as well as envisions success — will ultimately fail. Such wisdom is not restricted only to large-scale projects such as bridge-building. It also applies to the day-to-day administration of our tasks, our careers, and our lives, for they are also projects.

The I-Beam Review represents project planning within the context of time management, and is therefore the figurehead for this chapter, which focuses on planning and structure. Simply put, the I-Beam Review formalizes the planning process by insisting that each day be bracketed by a short planning session. Thus, the I-beam shape. These planning sessions need not be long — merely 15 minutes at the start of the day and 15 minutes at the end — but they will help ensure that the entire day is as practical and time-efficient as you want it to be.

Here is a sample day schedule that includes an I-Beam Review at the start and the end of the day.

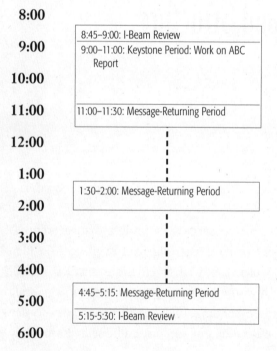

The top of the I-beam allows you to plan for the day. This quarter hour serves as a heads-up. It awakens your mind to what's on tap for the next eight to ten hours. The middle of the I-beam, represented by the dotted line, is the "spine" of your day, during which you have your meetings, work, take breaks, perform your tasks — all of which are allotted their proper time and are followed through upon their thorough completion. The bottom of the I-beam allows for "post-planning" of the day just past, as well as pre-planning for the two days to come. It is your opportunity to follow through on the actions of the entire day, ensuring that every activity has been completed and accounted for and that follow-up activities are properly scheduled.

Most people already go though some sort of plan at the beginning of each day, but the morning I-Beam Review formalizes this procedure, and helps you to

- identify your number-one-priority task
- assign your number-one-priority task to your Keystone Period
- schedule your Keystone Period
- reprioritize other tasks
- delegate irrelevant tasks
- schedule time for return phone calls and e-mail
- ensure your calendar is up-to-date on screen or on paper
- think through and anticipate Cool Time travel plans (see Chapter 8)
- put the tasks of the day in perspective to ensure that no time is spent on unnecessary or less valuable activities
- sow the seeds of crisis management (A crisis that comes at you from left field is much easier to handle if you know what gets put aside to accommodate it.)
- enable negotiations when tasks conflict (It is much easier to engage your intelligent push-back and establish a win-win

resolution if you can demonstrate a tangible, full schedule on screen or on paper.)

At the end of the day, invest 15 minutes in the act of post-planning. This allows you to

- get a heads-up for what's coming up in the next two days; and
- update and clean up the agenda for the day just past to make sure nothing is forgotten, to roll over unfinished tasks, and to ensure that the start and end times of the day's appointments are clear and accurate.

Restaurant Success: Great Cuisine and a Kitchen That's Clean!

Can you imagine how your favorite restaurant would look if the entire staff went home immediately after the last patron departed? In fact, a restaurant doesn't end its day until the kitchen is cleaned and utensils are prepped for the day to come.

That's what the I-Beam Review does for you: it's a preparation for the next day. It's a placement of mental tools and priorities, allowing you to hit your stride effectively in the morning.

Don't consider your workday over until the actions at the bottom of the I-beam have been performed. This requires that you put the last 15 minutes at the office aside for undisturbed planning. It means fighting the temptation to take on one more piece of work or return one more phone call. It means you must consider yourself to have "officially left the office," even though you are physically still there. No new work or calls; just tidying, wrapping up, and preparing for the next day.

Every person's life is different. It is up to you to determine how best to fit an I-beam structure into your day. But do it. Try it. Envision it and enforce it. Develop a mindset in which no day must pass by without an I-Beam Review.

Let's now look at other time management techniques that will go hand in hand with your twice-daily I-Beam Review. Remember: It's all about planning and structure.

Regarding Time Management as Project Management in Miniature

Project management, which has been around as a formalized school of thought and study since the 1950s, emphasizes the importance of planning, communication, performance, and review. The "home" of project management is the Project Management Institute (www.PMI.org), which publishes a work known as the *Project Management Body of Knowledge* or *PMBOK*. The intent of the *PMBOK* is to assist project managers everywhere, regardless of their experience, by providing a standard and a logical plan for the successful completion of projects.

Project management forces you to visualize a project from start to end. It allows you to plan for contingencies and revisions. It allows for forward and backward planning of activities, and ensures that the traditional "seat-of-the-pants" approach is replaced by an organized, accountable agenda.

There are five phases in traditional project management:

1. **Initiation.** In this phase, the project is conceived and assessed as viable or not; ideas are formulated; and the expected results and timeline are first considered.
2. **Planning.** A large part of the project's life is spent here — sometimes the bulk of it. Every detail of the project should be accounted for to the finest degree, including possible failures, contingencies, estimated times for completion of each part, and budget and resource estimates.
3. **Execution.** The project gets underway, people start to work on the project, and momentum begins.

4. **Control.** The work of the project is performed while the project manager oversees and updates the plan and communicates progress and changes to all involved.
5. **Closure.** Once the project is completed — successfully or not — the project teams are broken up, final accounting is done, and things are cleaned up and put away.

The project is summarized and guided by a *project plan*, a document that lays out tasks and their respective timelines throughout the life of the project. Far from being a static document, the project plan must be flexible, a "living, breathing thing," which can adapt to changes while still allowing the project to move ahead.

In short, project management makes everything as clear as it can possibly be and envisions all aspects of the project before they happen. It does not necessarily make a project effortless, but its principles and rules ensure that work and resources are properly guided. The planning phase allows for an educated degree of foresight while the closure phase allows for hindsight, which in itself serves as the foresight for future projects.

Furthermore, project management helps plan for contingencies and emergencies. It counteracts some major time wasters by clearly defining the roles and expectations of everyone involved. It avoids confused responsibility and maintains a chain of communication, so team members know whom to call if problems arise. It allows you to see where you are going, which in turn allows for safer mid-course corrections.

What does this have to do with time management? Everything. Project management is central to effective time management, since each task you undertake is really a project in miniature. Furthermore, each day should be seen as a project composed of micro-projects. Your calendar year, your current career, your life — these are macro-projects. If you visualize everything as a project, you can use the components of project management to achieve your goals successfully. The same procedures that help build bridges and buildings can be applied to your day, and can structure and control your activities for your benefit.

Understanding the Critical Path

In project management, the *critical path* is defined as the shortest possible timeline by which all component tasks of a project must be completed. If any one of the tasks is delayed by a day, or even a few hours, each successive task will have to be bumped down, and the project will end late, just like the boxcars of a freight train. A wise project manager factors a few "slack" periods into a project to allow for the unexpected. A task that is estimated to take two days will be project-planned as needing three, so that if something untoward were to happen, the task could be delayed an entire day without affecting the project.

It's not wise to work to the critical path, since this leaves no room for error. It is wise, however, to identify the critical path of a project so as to be able to plan back from its due date, allowing and inserting plenty of room for errors and revisions.

An example of the benefits of identifying a project's critical path, then expanding to allow for the inevitable, would be that of preparing a presentation to be given on the 30th of next month. Suppose we start by listing the steps involved, together with an optimistic duration for each:

Task	Date
Create the slides for the presentation.	26th
Run through and proof the presentation.	27th

Task	Date (cont'd)
Get approval for the presentation.	27th
Send slide show to printers	
for creation of color overheads.	27th
Print, collate, and staple handouts.	27th
Pick up slide-show overheads from printers.	28th
Rehearse presentation.	29th
Pack handouts and overheads.	29th
Give presentation.	30th

Wow. Looks pretty good! You won't have to get started on this until the 26th. Or so it seems. But in truth, this is the critical path, and to work to this schedule means that the slightest delay — say, for example, in getting the approval for the presentation from your manager — will slow down production, which will either require postponement of the presentation, or a long evening spent at an all-night copy shop, neither of which is terribly attractive.

By pragmatically extending these durations, you build in grace time, which will certainly be needed and used. An amended production schedule might instead look something like this:

Task	Date	Reason
Create the slides for the presentation.	15th	Design always takes longer than you'd think.
Run through and proof the presentation.	20th	Proofing always takes longer than you'd think. Allow a couple of days in between other tasks.
Get approval for the presentation.	22nd	In case approval authority is absent on the 23rd.

Task	Date	Reason (cont'd)
Send slide show to printers for creation of color overheads.	24th	Allow plenty of time for production and corrections.
Print, collate, and staple handouts.	27th	
Pick up slide-show overheads from printers.	28th	
Rehearse presentation.	28th	In case the 29th gets too busy.
Pack handouts and overheads.	29th	
Give presentation.	30th	

Obviously you would not be working on this project all day, every day, between the 15th and the 30th — in fact, this schedule gives you plenty of time to focus on your other tasks. What this schedule also gives you is a calm and controlled method of preparing for an upcoming activity.

This is why project management is so important to time management. By taking the time up front to plan the project, think through the steps, and allow realistic padding to the component tasks, you will remain in control of not only this project, but the rest of your day as well.

Prioritizing

What if, one day, you were walking down a suburban street and you saw a man frantically bailing water out of his rapidly flooding basement? You ask the man, "Why don't you call Public Works and have them shut the water off until you find the leak?", to which the man replies, "I can't do that now. I've got all this water to get rid of."

Obviously, this person has a problem with prioritization that is starting to cloud his judgment. Yet this analogy is not so far-flung from the day-to-day tribulations of many working professionals. The floodwater in their case is the endless river of mail, phone calls, meetings, distractions, and work that just keeps on coming. We take on each task as it comes in an earnest attempt to beat down the tide, with no time given to assess the relative importance of that task.

In the flooded basement parable above, it is easy to observe the situation from the cool, detached Bird's-Eye View of a dispassionate observer and note that, if he had chosen to call the city, the man could have saved himself hours of wasted labor. It's very difficult, however, to adopt that cool perspective when the flood is happening to us. A lot of people will work instead on a conveyor-belt approach, taking each task as it comes in a vain attempt to get to the bottom of the pile.

But that's exactly where you must go — up to the vantage point of the Bird's-Eye View (see Chapter 6). Next time your inbox piles up with tasks, deadlines, and conflicting requests, take a brief minute or so to step back and review. Remember our man in his flooded basement, and recall the value of reprioritizing. Avoid the urge to "get started" just long enough to make sure you're getting started on the right thing — prioritization before action.

As you plan your day according to your I-Beam Review, as you assign yourself your Keystone Period, and especially as new tasks come in and demand your

---

Medic!

Have you heard the term *triage*? In medical terminology it refers to the technique of sorting out a group of injured people into three categories (hence the term *tri-age*) so that the most serious cases are treated first or by the appropriate specialist. The three categories are:

- those who will survive if given immediate medical help;
- those who will survive with medical help, but can wait a little while; and
- those who won't survive.

In our corporate world, most decisions are not literally life or death; however, they still may have an impact on the life (or death) of our careers or projects – and thus the pressure to tackle several conflicting tasks simultaneously still exists.

attention, ensure they all fall into place according to priority.

The graphic below illustrates the priority chart. It has been used for years and can be found in many time management and organization manuals, with good reason. It is a practical method for assessing and processing conflicting tasks, both during your I-Beam Review and in a period of crisis. Every task should fall into one of these quadrants:

- Urgent and Priority
- Urgent but Not Priority
- Priority but Not Urgent
- Not Urgent and Not Priority

Sometimes it helps to fall back on this priority chart, since it removes some of the guilt you might feel when deciding which task to take over any other task. The use of the priority chart becomes part of your Emotional Bedrock (see Chapter 11). It enables you to say "No" to additional tasks by applying a neutral yet proven decision-making device, instead of giving in to external pressures or suffering the confusion and stress brought on when too many tasks appear simultaneously.

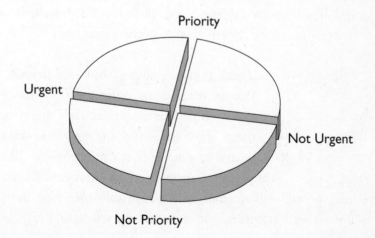

The priority chart helps you to categorize every task into one of the following four sections:

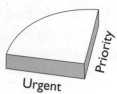

The task that is both urgent and priority. This refers to the task that can, should, and must be done by you — *now*. It is directly related to your immediate goals and is clearly most important. It should be scheduled right away. There should only be one urgent and priority task facing you at any given time, since there is only one of you. Other tasks may appear almost as high in priority, but the effective time manager recognizes that only one task at a time can be number one.

Tasks that are priority but not as urgent. These tasks must also be done pretty soon, but when you step back and review all of the tasks in front of you, they come second in order of priority. Perhaps they can be delegated, or at least scheduled for later in the day or the week. A regular revisitation to your Active Agenda (see Chapter 5) and your I-Beam Review will ensure that these items do not slip into temporary obscurity only to emerge as crises later on.

Tasks that are urgent but not priority. People often have difficulty recognizing these types of tasks, even though they face them every day. How can any task that's related to your work not be a priority? The most obvious examples of Urgent but Not Priority tasks are e-mail, postal mail, memos, and phone calls. Most of these will need your attention, but must they have it right away? As

I discuss in Chapter 2, time management is about assigning specific times throughout the day to address these types of Urgent but Not Priority activities. They are to be dealt with during scheduled message-returning periods, not necessarily immediately and in the order of their arrival.

Other Urgent but Not Priority tasks might also come your way in the form of work that is urgent to someone else, but not to you — or work that was unexpected, its very existence throwing you temporarily for a loop. The technique here is not to give in to panic and get "stuck" into the new task, but to step back and assess its priority with the understanding that working in Cool Time is more productive and healthy than working in a frenzy.

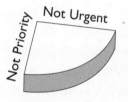

Tasks that are neither urgent nor priority. These tasks are the lowest on the totem pole. They may carry a certain amount of importance in and of themselves, but attending to them may have to wait, or better yet, be assigned to someone else. There is just not enough time to take on everything that comes your way, and attempting to handle tasks of low priority, especially before higher priority tasks, is a key time management problem.

Perhaps, as you take your Bird's-Eye View (see Chapter 6) of your upcoming week, you may wish to assign an hour or two per week to deal with these non-urgent, non-priority tasks. Of course, this depends on your schedule and on what these tasks may entail, but the principle remains the same: don't let these low-level obligations leak out and destroy the productive potential of your work time.

If you're having trouble deciding whether a task could or

should be demoted to Not Urgent and/or Not Priority, take a moment to ask yourself a few questions about the task:

- Does this task contribute to the main reason why I'm here in this job, at this company?
- If I don't do this task immediately, will the resulting trouble be greater than the gains I expect to achieve from the task I'm currently doing?
- Will this task that I'm doing matter a year from now?
- What if I don't do this task at all?

These questions are not intended to justify procrastination or avoidance, but are instead to help you avoid falling into the "80/20 principle," described next.

The 80/20 Principle

The 80/20 principle is a descriptive device used to illustrate many areas of human activity. Within the realm of time management and prioritization, this principle relates to the ratio of work to achievement, and can be viewed from two perspectives:

Eighty percent of our time is spent on things that yield only 20 percent of our value. In other words, we spend far too much time on activities that are comparatively worthless. Examples abound, and their solutions are often nearby, hidden just out of sight. Such activities include commuting; spending two hours or more a day sitting in traffic; waiting in line at bank machines, in food courts, and in transit stations; and trying to fix software, a jammed copier, or a problematic e-mail attachment. Many of these activities are important to our day and cannot be eliminated. But they can be refined.

Rather than spend half your lunch hour standing in line at a bank machine with everyone else, for example, why not go in the late afternoon, when everyone else is back at work? The entire trip would take just a few minutes — shorter, I dare say, than a colleague's cigarette break. Perhaps you could choose a commute time just prior to or just after rush hour, and stagger your work hours accordingly.

> **Fire Your Weakest Customer**
>
> Many business gurus will tell you that in terms of the 80/20 principle, 80 percent of your business will come from 20 percent of your client base. So, not only must you focus on your top 20 percent (customers that bring you the most business, projects that do the most for your career), but you must also regularly jettison those that are doing little or nothing for you.
>
> That's hard for any professional to do, whether you're self-employed or part of a team. But projects that interfere with more profitable endeavors result in lost time, lost opportunity, lost profits.
>
> By taking a regular Bird's-Eye view, you will be able to regain perspective and clearly recognize the work that offers the most value – as well as the work that's slowing you down.

Twenty percent of our work yields 80 percent of our value. This phrase looks at work rather than time, and states that there is a fraction of your work — one fifth, the tip of the iceberg — that yields the greatest productivity and/or profit for you. It makes sense, therefore, to identify, isolate, and focus on those activities rather than leaving them mixed in with the less valuable tasks. The path to effective time management and its resultant benefits starts once again with planning: taking some time to assess and prioritize. Regularly take a Bird's-Eye View and ensure that every minute of every day is being applied intelligently to those tasks and priorities that will achieve personal progress, balance, and satisfaction.

The SMARTS Test

This formula springs from the pages of project management, and will help assess the validity and priority of a task. The SMARTS test is used by project managers to assess every part of a project well before embarking on the tasks at hand. You may wish to consider applying the SMARTS test to your I-Beam Review, to ensure that the tasks you assign to yourself — or even those that someone else may assign to you — are truly worth your time and effort.

First, have a look at how the SMARTS test applies to projects within classic project management:

- **Specific.** Is the task definite? Is it an identifiable task, or a more vague collection of subtasks? "Buy a loaf of brown bread" is specific. "Ensure the pantry is stocked" is not specific.
- **Measurable.** Can you measure the task? How can you tell when the task is complete? When does it start? When does it end? "Get the company Web site up and running" is not a measurable task. Does the Web site project end when the site goes live? What about ongoing maintenance, updates, and corrections? Is that part of the project, or is it a separate project? What are the metrics that clearly define the parameters of this task?
- **Achievable.** Can this task be done? Is it possible? If you ask me to personally perform a forensic audit on a now-defunct company, and I am not qualified to perform any sort of accounting services, then the task is not achievable no matter how much money or time you offer me.
- **Realistic.** Let's suppose, using the forensic accounting example above, that I am qualified to do this work. The task is possible and achievable, but if you want the report on your desk in two days — even though I'm occupied with another

case, and no money or staff can be assigned to assist — the satisfactory completion of this task is not realistic.

- **Time-oriented.** Is there a schedule, a timeline, a deadline for the completion of the task? This ties in closely with the "measurable" principle, in that I'll need to know not only what defines the start and end of a project, but also what the dates for starting, ending, reviewing, delivery, etc. are. Without written timelines, it's easy for a task to drift.
- **Signed-off.** To whom do I report? Who is the person that approves this project, who will be authorized to accept the finished product, and to whom should all questions and issues be directed? Who am I working for on this project?

The SMARTS test ensures that before any work is done, there is a clear understanding of the scope and the parameters of the work involved. We see these concepts echo in so many areas of time management, such as in meetings, where we insist that every person must be clear on the next step and who is to perform it; and in the concepts of the I-Beam Review and the Bird's-Eye View (see Chapter 6), in which we "step back" briefly before moving ahead in order to assess the territory.

Now, if you take these terms and apply them to time management, and more specifically to the tasks that are currently crowding your calendar, you get this:

- **Specific.** As you review the task in front of you, make sure you have a clear understanding of what exactly it is. Where does it start? Where does it end? What happens next? The more specific you are about the things you have to do, the better you will be able to estimate their durations, including travel times, breathing times, and Cool Time (see Chapter 8). Being specific about your tasks starts the thinking process in your head, allowing you to run through the task, envision possible obstacles and problems, and prepare yourself for them before they happen.

- **Measurable.** What are the beginning and ending milestones of this task? How will you know when the task is complete? For some tasks this is obvious, but tasks lacking a true definition can take far more time than they're worth (remember Parkinson's Law: work expands to fill the time available). Can you report back and prove to yourself and to your manager/client that the task is complete so that you can follow through and move on to the next task?

- **Achievable.** Can this task actually be done? Is it something you can do? Are you qualified to do this task? People have an inherent optimism that tends to overestimate their abilities. Optimism is good, of course, but it's a positive energy that must be channeled toward truly productive activities; otherwise, it will pour out uncontrolled, like spilled milk. Think for a moment. In a world where you had nothing else to do except for this project, would you be able to do it, or should someone else be assigned? The wise time manager knows when to delegate.

- **Realistic.** Even if you assess the task as one you could conceivably do, what else do you have on your plate right now? We all have to balance many responsibilities simultaneously; our jobs and our corporate culture make that compulsory. Therefore, is the task at hand realistic, given everything else you have to do?

- **Time-oriented.** Can you see the beginning and the end of the task in your mind? Can you see it on paper? Is it scheduled for the most productive or appropriate time of your day and your year? Is there a deadline you can plan toward?

- **Signed-off.** To whom do you report? Who is the person that approves this project, and who will accept it upon completion?

Set Priorities for the Day and Do Number One First

As living beings, we have metabolic ups and downs throughout the day. We cannot operate at maximum output for eight or ten hours straight — our bodies and minds were not designed for that. In short, there is a certain time of the day when we are at our metabolic peak, where memory, attentiveness, alertness, and energy are at a high point — though they will dwindle as the day moves along. For most people, this peak is in the morning, between 9:00 and 9:30. Others, however, may not peak until 11:00, others at 4:00, and still others between 10:00 p.m. and midnight. In addition, our personal peaks may occur at different times on different days, depending on stress levels, the quality of sleep the night before, what we eat, and even the time of year.

Our work environments generally pay little heed to this metabolic roller coaster. With the exception of the lunch period — to which everyone is entitled, and of which everyone should take full advantage — much of our day has the potential to remain unstructured, like an empty table upon which are piled meetings, tasks, phone calls, travel, research, and more, in whichever order they arrive.

The efficient time manager, however, sees great potential in combining three time management elements for maximized productivity and personal success, as follows.

As you perform your I-Beam Review, identify the most important task for the day, your number-one priority, and assign it

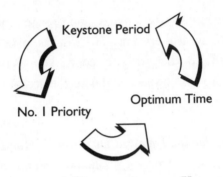

to your Keystone Period. Then, assign your Keystone Period to that part of the day when you personally are at your best.

This may not be possible to implement overnight. There are meetings and projects scheduled with other people that can't be rescheduled this quickly. This technique will require phasing in over the weeks to follow. Identify when your peak period is. Get used to the rhythms of your own metabolism, and much like a surfer, time your actions to get the most from the next wave.

You stand a better chance of making this work if your peak period and Keystone Period are scheduled for early morning. People often hit a stumbling block here, by identifying their number-one priority but then getting caught up in other things throughout the day, so that this highest priority task still remains unstarted by 4:00 p.m. Why? Distractions, time-eaters, crises, new issues, and new tasks devour the day, filling up your two-pound bucket with gaping holes of wasted time.

But when you implement and take advantage of the triumvirate of number-one priority, peak period, and Keystone Period, you wield a powerful tool for success.

Scheduling Work for the "Trough Period"
The flip side to doing your number-one item while still at your best is dealing with activities and events that are scheduled for

the "trough" period in the mid-afternoon, when you and others will certainly not be in peak form. Understanding that this problem exists, and taking measures to counteract it, is another tool to help maximize your productivity throughout the entire 24-hour day.

This concept is discussed in more detail in "The Dynamics of the Day" (see Chapter 10). In a nutshell, the period of early to mid-afternoon, from 2:00 to 3:30 p.m., is a time at which the body is at its lowest physical ebb of the entire waking day and even the simplest tasks seem to require increased effort. This is due to a combination of factors, including the fact that your body is busy digesting its lunch while simultaneously mirroring the metabolic ebb of the deep-sleep period of 2:00 to 3:30 a.m.

It is crucial, therefore, to take into account that you, your colleagues, and your clients will all be a little drowsy during this time.

Since this trough period makes up a large portion of the entire working day, it is a constraint we are forced to work with. If you have to attend or chair a meeting during this period — or worse, if you are scheduled to give a speech or presentation — ensure your participants have plenty of opportunities to get up, move around, and stretch. Give them access to fresh air, refreshments, and natural light. Whatever your afternoon activities may be, structure them so that natural breaks occur. Soldiering on in the name of gritty determination may show strength of spirit, but the quality of the work will suffer.

As you perform your I-Beam Review and plan individual projects, remain aware that you are not a machine, and neither you nor your manager can expect otherwise. As you estimate the duration of an upcoming task, stand firm on the Emotional Bedrock of physiology. Any human being, regardless of talent, dexterity, dedication, or intelligence, is working on an unstable metabolic platform that dips and wavers gradually downward toward sleep. Only by understanding and working within these constraints can productive, time-efficient work be completed.

Taking On More Than You Can Handle

People often lose control over their lives when they take on too much, or when someone else has assigned them too much. It often starts with an inability or a reluctance to recognize the limitations inherent in our selves and in our day, and it ends with stress, crisis, and overload. Remember, the figurehead of this chapter is an I-beam, which represents the application of project management principles to your day. Project management is about planning, assessment, and the use of guidelines, more so than about effort. As individuals, the temptation to take on more than is possible must be carefully monitored and controlled. Examples of how this unchanneled optimism infiltrates our minds include the following:

The Superhero Complex

This complex comes from a self-imposed feeling, especially among overly ambitious people, that you must do it all — that you can be a productive, overachieving professional taking on all the roles of a project, while also acting as an excellent nurturing parent and a socially active citizen. You expect to enjoy a balanced, fulfilling relationship with your partner, while simultaneously driving your career forward and upward. The need to prove these things to yourself and to others may seem admirable, but it is also self-defeating.

The secret to success in both time management and personal management is in knowing your constraints and maximizing your productivity in league with them, rather than attempting the same in spite of them. Recognizing that gap between what we wish to be and what we can be is not a depressing or defeatist action. Honestly, it's not! In fact, it is constructive, allowing you to build self-awareness on a more solid foundation, your Emotional Bedrock (see Chapter 11). By recognizing and working within the constraints of your existence, and by allowing balance and nutrition to take a role in your life on par with your ambitions and feelings of responsibility, you will be able to achieve a great deal more of your goals.

Learn to delegate, identify, and perform only the tasks that are best suited to your talents and goals. Flashy superhero stuff should be left to fictional characters. Your success will come from the diligent, intelligent application of your time and energies to carefully chosen, high-value tasks, with time for rest and balance in between.

Overconfidence

Whereas the superhero complex is the belief that you must do it all, overconfidence takes that further and suggests there's nothing you can't do. Though that's great for the ego, at least initially, the stress of trying to keep up with the demands of an over-enthusiastic psyche can be damaging. Overconfidence is best when channeled. By taking the time to regularly perform a Bird's-Eye View (see Chapter 6), and by diligently planning your day, the energy that comes from overconfidence can remain the blessing that it is, rather than becoming a millstone. Focus your talents on realistic, attainable goals rather than spreading yourself so thin that all your projects starve. In the words of Publius Syrus (42 BC), "Never promise more than you can perform."

Failure to Delegate

This a major reason for taking on too much. Whether it stems from the fear that others cannot do the job as well as you can or simply from not thinking about it, failure to delegate becomes a major time-waster, as it channels your energy, talent, and time deep into the dark side of the 80/20 principle. Sometimes, believe it or not, there are people who are both able and available to do something better than you. When that happens, it's best to leave it with them. Other times, you may have to give a portion of a project over to someone less qualified, which is less appealing and may require a little more supervision or time to complete. In that case, it's a judgment call. So long as the work that you should really be doing is of higher value than the work you are delegating, then the math is on your side. When you have to delegate to less qualified people, this is a project constraint (see Chapter 10 for more on constraints). Accept it, plan around it, and continue with your own work. Failure to delegate fills your two-pound bucket with gaps, and your day is already too short for that.

Having No One to Delegate To

Understaffing leads to a shortage of capable people, yet workloads continue to increase. This time management situation is more difficult to rectify and is a prime reason why people take on too much. In this case, the issue of taking on too much is imposed from outside, rather than being a specific, internal personality trait. To this I have a one-word response: "Why?"

Why is there no one to delegate to? Can your company not afford to hire extra staff? That's a reasonable answer. But why, then, is the existing staff expected to do the work of those missing people? In many cases, the answer is along the lines of "Because it has to get done." It's a lot easier to have willing, patient staff take on the extra responsibility than it is to take a Bird's-Eye View of the company's abilities and obligations and plan or re-plan accordingly. Maybe the reason is more internal, in that you yourself are reluctant to say "No" to additional tasks.

Basically, one must fight unreasonable workload with clearly documented schedules and calendars that allow senior management to see and understand that you are working at your most efficient. This is the essence of the intelligent push-back. Simply buckling under and taking on the additional workload willingly — or through some sense of "If I don't do it, who will?" — sends a message, a dangerous message, that this additional workload can be handled by you and is therefore not unreasonable. From that point on, people will expect the same level of work from you and the bar will continue to be raised.

Advocating these principles is not a call for a work-to-rule, or any other type of labor-related resistance. It demonstrates that on many levels, time management is not simply an internal, personal technique, but instead is one that requires the buy-in, vision, and participation of colleagues and superiors.

Unrealistic Time Estimates

Taking on too much work can also be the unintentional result of underestimating how long a task will take. This echoes and magnifies my discussion of the critical path, where, if one task goes on overly long, it will crash into the start of the next task, resulting once again in crisis and overwork.

Estimating a task is a difficult and inexact science, which is why so much of project management focuses on the importance of planning, re-planning, and allowing slack times between tasks so as not to get trapped on the critical path. And one thing's for sure: a task will always take longer than you think. So to start with, when you have to estimate the duration of a task, take your gut instinct, double it, and add half again.

Double it and half again? That's pretty unrealistic, isn't it? Well, it's a matter of factoring in the unexpected. Perhaps a key resource is missing. Maybe the document you're writing will be sent back for edits and clarifications. Perhaps a top-priority phone call comes in, one that mustn't be ignored. The point is that things seldom, if ever, take the amount of time you hope they would. They always take more.

By factoring in this extra time in the first place, you stand a better chance of completing the task within realistic timelines. If all goes well, and you finish before you expected, you'll have time left over for other tasks and you'll feel (and look) like a hero. If things take a little longer, however, it's healthy and smart to have that cushion time. Use your SMARTS formula to determine whether the task whose duration you are trying to estimate is truly *a* task, or in

The PERT Technique

If you think all this focus on "double it and add half again" seems half-baked, you may be interested to learn that estimating task durations has been part of formalized project management since the U.S. Navy's development of its Polaris missile program in the early 1960s, as well as DuPont's cement-factory building projects in that same era. They included a calculation for estimating job durations that went like this:

P = Pessimistic: how long the project would take if almost everything had problems

O = Optimistic: how long the project would take if everything went perfectly

R = Realistic: how long the project will probably take, based on the estimates of experienced project managers

The formula to calculate expected duration of the project then became

$$\frac{O + 4R + P}{6}$$

Now that's rocket science!

fact a *series* of tasks. If it is the latter, planning, diagrams, or project management software may be a time-efficient tactic. By planning proactively, you will be able to fend off stress, keeping your higher-level faculties focused on producing top-quality work. You'll be working in Cool Time.

Failure and Contingency: Proactive Time Management

All our lives, we have been taught that failure is wrong, failure is bad. It started when we were infants. For most of us, the first negative emotional experience to come our way was the first time Mom said "No." From that moment on, we were confined to a world of rules, a world of power structures and negotiation. The seeds of being "right" or being "wrong" were planted on that day. Subsequent years in school and at work echoed this message and forged the rigid principles of acceptable behavior and achievement.

Words such as "no," "wrong," "bad," and "failure" sting our conscience and can hold us back from doing the things we really would like to do. If we try, we might fail, and when we fail, we see ourselves as wrong and bad. The flaw in this argument is in the definition of the word "failure."

In project management terms, when you plan a project, there can be no failures. There can only be alternate outcomes with their own sets of results. Alternate outcomes are learning opportunities. An experiment that explodes in the lab isn't a failure; it teaches us something that wasn't previously known about the elements being mixed, which will contribute to the effectiveness of the next experiment. When alternate outcomes are planned for, you have contingencies. And with contingency planning, you have proactive time management.

The relevance that this has to day-to-day time management is direct: a clear vision of the day and its tasks saves time and improves productivity in and of itself. When contingencies are factored into the plan, crises can be averted or at least dealt with properly. Contingency planning avoids stress and increases achievement through proper planning and anticipation of problems. Things that do not go exactly according to Plan A can be dealt with through Plan B or Plan C.

In short, the word "failure," in project management terms, does not equal the term "wrong." It is an alternate outcome that can be anticipated and dealt with.

As you perform your day-to-day I-Beam Review, take a moment to factor in contingencies for your major activities. Ask yourself, "If this doesn't work, what can be done instead?" In the sections on creating a precedent checklist (see Chapter 9) and the critical path, you can see that extra days are allowed for procedures such as obtaining approval and printing. Why so much extra time? To allow for contingencies should the slides come out wrong, or should modifications be required. The stress, errors, and costs involved in last-minute, seat-of-the-pants efforts to rectify panic situations are very preventable with contingency planning.

By factoring contingency into your professional and personal life, you are practicing proactive time management by anticipating problems before they happen and being ready for them. Take the time to plan for the things you don't want to happen. It will turn out to be far less than the time spent dealing with unexpected crises.

Fire Safety

A dramatic yet worthwhile discussion of contingency planning concerns fire safety. What does that have to do with time management? Pretty much everything, given the potential for loss in time, loss of material goods, reconstruction of data, and worse, loss of life.

Practice fire safety on the road. Next time you check into a hotel, on business or on vacation, be sure to note the fire exit stairwell closest to your room, and then count the number of door-

Who Is Your Fire Warden?

Do you know the name of the fire warden for your floor or department? Who is the person charged with ensuring all staff leave the floor safely and quickly? At my seminars, about 50 percent of participants don't know – though 100 percent of them should.

way recesses between your room and that stairwell. Does that seem silly? It may save your life, should you find yourself on hands and knees in a smoke-filled hallway, in a strange building, in a strange town, in the middle of the night.

Practice fire safety at home. When was the last time you had a full fire drill with your family? Most families have little in the way of contingency planning for an emergency escape. Examples of this sort of planning include understanding the importance of feeling a door for heat before opening it; moving around on hands and knees; being able to escape from a second-floor bedroom window; rescuing pets; having phones, flashlights, and valuables nearby; and giving children clear instructions on where to regroup. Planning for a fire may seem embarrassing or even morbid in the light of day, but it may make a major difference should the situation occur.

Obviously, there are many other instances of pre-planning you could consider at this moment. The idea here is twofold. First, take the fire-safety concerns to heart. Second, use them as a metaphor for the importance of contingency planning for all of your undertakings at the office. Proactive, preemptive time management is always a smart use of your time, no matter what the situation.

What to Do When a Key Player Is Unavailable

When you have to count on people other than yourself to perform tasks within a project, you leave yourself open to many possible problems, one of which is the possibility that they might not be available precisely when you need them the most. No one works the same, thinks the same, or holds the same priorities as you do, and they can't be expected to. There may be numerous reasons for a professional staff member to suddenly become unavailable, from family emergencies to personal illness to conflicting priorities at work. I'm not advocating the elimination of teamwork, here — in fact, the synergy derived from numerous minds working on a common goal most often far outweighs the problems inherent in the procedure. However, people are their own masters, even if they are working under your guidance or employ. They are constraints to your project.

What would ensue, therefore, if a member of your staff or project team didn't show up tomorrow? Where would you be then? Where would the project be? When I ask this question of most people, they shudder slightly and describe their strategy this way: "I really hope that doesn't happen."

The efficient time manager must learn to skirt this problem by having a contingency plan. Who could replace this missing person? Is there enough slack time built into the project plan that the person's absence could be tolerated for a few days without moving the entire project onto the critical path? Planning in advance with an eye to such troubles is the only way to efficiently manage your time when you are counting on others to help you through. In other words, count on them not being there and build your foundations from that point. Remember, an ounce of prevention is worth a pound of cure.

Pay Me Now or Pay Me Later

If none of the above holds any water with you, there is one principle that describes the importance of contingency planning in a nutshell: the phrase "pay me now or pay me later." It is a hard thing for people to accept that the task they are planning or are currently working on will take longer and will require more effort than they are willing to put in. This is not due to laziness, but to the fact that there are other tasks, deadlines, and pressures waiting to be addressed, and they've all got to get done. But it *will* take longer. You either put in the resources up front, or you wait until it comes back, at which point it fights for space with your next task. This concept is also referred to in discussing the importance of rest and leisure within your 24-hour day for the same reason (see Chapter 7): something improperly done will require redoing.

As you perform your I-Beam Review, as you take your Bird's-Eye View (see Chapter 6), and as you draw up your project plans, remember that sufficient time invested in advance helps avoid returns, repeats, and crises later.

Strategic Timing

A key planning and structure technique that is overlooked by many people is that of strategic timing: taking advantage of quiet zones in the day, the week, and the year to perform tasks more efficiently, with less stress and time wasted. I make mention of this in the discussion of the 80/20 principle, above, in which 80 percent of our time is spent on things that offer 20 percent of the day's value. Now, given that everybody's life is different, some of the following suggestions may not be directly applicable. Then again, maybe they could be, if you tweak them ever so slightly to match your work and life priorities.

- **Food shopping.** Do you crowd into the supermarket on a Saturday or a Thursday evening to do your food shopping with the rest of the world? Consider the possibility of rescheduling your shopping to a different night of the week, or shopping for staple goods once a month, or subscribing to a supermarket or Internet-based food delivery service to have the goods shipped directly to your door.
- **Seasonal shopping.** Everyone swears they'll never leave holiday shopping to the last minute ever again, but most of us proceed to do it all over again the following year. Could you spread your holiday shopping out over a few weeks well before the crunch period? Build your gift-giving list up over the year as you hear hints being dropped or comments made by deserving family members. Standard items such as a bottle of champagne for New Year's Eve, for example, could be purchased in November, eliminating the need to stand in line.
- **Banking.** Bank tellers and bank machines are busiest at lunchtime, on Fridays, and at the end of the month. Plan your day, week, and month accordingly to capitalize on those times of the day when line-ups are shorter or nonexistent.
- **Commuting.** Time spent in a car or on transit systems at rush hour is time lost on a grand scale. Anything that can be done to avoid losing time in commuting purgatory should be actively pursued. Is it possible for you to work from home one or two days a week? Is it possible for you to modify your hours, arriving at work at a time other than the norm? Can you arrange to leave from work at different times as well?

Or, is it possible to arrange a "working car pool" in which cell phones, portable computers, and wireless e-mail allow for work to be done while on the way to work? This method really does work, but it requires buy-in from all participants, of course, and that small talk be kept to a minimum. Participants take turns in sending outgoing calls, so as to not all talk at once, and one participant takes care of e-mail and other tasks for the driver. Not only does it get the day off to a productive start, but also it reduces tension and stress by turning gridlock into a productive work time.

In sum, is there a way you can take a second look at these time-consuming activities, with an eye to improving them? Naturally, constraints such as family, pets, and non-work activities factor into your plans, but many people live and work on the spur of the moment. They don't get the Bird's-Eye view, which is a shame, because things are so much clearer up there.

Strategic Vacation Planning

Most everyone looks forward to their vacation, and rightly so. This is supposed to be the time of relaxation and recharging. It's essential for maintaining balance. Your vacation should be treated as one of the most important parts of your job, because that's just what it is. But before you go, take some time to plan your vacation period carefully, to help ensure a smooth, stress-free departure — and more importantly, a smooth, stress-free return.

Plan Ahead to Avoid the Pre-Vacation Crunch

The last few days at the office before a vacation can be the most stressful of all, as all the work that would have occupied three or four business days of the following week seems to become imme-diately top-priority and absolutely must get finished before your departure.

This situation is completely avoidable, since vacations rarely come as a surprise. Most vacation times are reserved many months in advance to ensure that everybody doesn't take off at the same time. Therefore, if you start planning your departure many months before the actual date, you should be able to influence the timelines of projects, meetings, and other office events with which the vacation may conflict.

As you maintain your Active Agenda (see Chapter 5), and as you step back and take a Bird's-Eye View of upcoming projects, draw a protective barrier around the period of your vacation, including the ten business days leading up to it and immediately following it. Make sure those days before your vacation are care-fully planned to hand off responsibilities to others or wrap up parts of a project. These days are not business as usual for you. If you try to keep working on your normal tasks at your normal pace on these days, you will generate more stress and overwork than the holiday could possibly alleviate.

Draw up a list of colleagues who can be counted on for per-forming small tasks on your behalf, such as returning a call to a key client, or ensuring delivery of a package on the first Monday of your holiday.

Set up instructions on your outgoing voice-mail message, and on your e-mail auto-reply, letting everyone know you'll be unavailable. Ask them to call back after a certain date rather than leave a message, and make this a date that is definitely *not* your first day back in the office. Avoid leaving a contact number at your vacation place for everyone's knowledge. If your position is such that you must be reachable for the highest-level emergency, leave your number with a trusted senior official. Remember, your rest and relaxation are of the utmost importance. Even if you thrive on daily contact, remember that the restorative properties of a properly run vacation will enhance your working abilities on your return.

Keep your priorities in view. Not all work is going to get finished by the time your holiday starts. Some things can wait or can be delegated. And you know what? The company will survive without you, at least for a couple of weeks. Avoid taking on additional projects during this time, since these activities will only cloud the enjoyment of your holiday. Remind people that you will soon be back, and that life will go on.

Give Your Phone a Holiday, Too

Your cell phone deserves a break as well. I recommend you keep it with you during holidays, but only for personal security or to keep in touch with family members. Use your phone as a holiday tool. Leave business at home.

Leave an Hour Early on the Last Day Before Your Vacation

This is pure self-indulgence, and it feels absolutely great, which in itself goes a long way toward establishing balance in your life and getting your vacation off on the right foot. Enjoy the freedom of that stolen hour. Definitely avoid working late on your holiday eve. Working late would rob you and your family of the good feeling that a holiday should bring. It is unfair and completely avoidable.

Plan Your Return Before You Leave

Though most people don't want to even think about their return to work as they start their holiday, a smooth return will help to ease the stress of stepping back into the rat race. Do not schedule meetings for that first day back after a vacation. You must allow this to be an ease-in day, in which much of the time is given over to catching up on the events that happened during your absence. Your Keystone Period for that day should consist of focusing on returning calls, updating your Active Agenda, and getting back up to speed. Keep the first day back from a holiday for you.

Why is this notion of keeping the first day back "for yourself" so important? Because too many people simply return to the office and hit the ground running, trying to immediately regain the pace they were at when they left. They return straight away to the stress levels and pressures that they left behind, and thus erase much of the therapeutic benefits that a vacation brings. Remember: Your vacation is a tool for relaxation and rebuilding. It is part of your job. You benefit, your family benefits, and your company benefits. Ease your way back into the rat race, and you will be better prepared to handle it. And of course, start planning your next vacation immediately!

Consider Spending Part of Your Vacation at Home

A two-week vacation in the Caribbean sounds great, but a ten-day island vacation bracketed by four days at home may be even more relaxing. Spending some time at home while everyone at the office thinks you're away gives you the time to get a few things done, to enjoy a certain quiet that the house seldom sees, to catch up on a few overdue tasks, and to put your mind at rest. A couple of days at home before you depart for your holiday trip, followed by a couple of days after, also allows you to prepare for your trip and travel to the airport in Cool Time, without stress, hurry, or forgetting anything.

The same applies to your return. Operating in Cool Time is especially important if you plan to travel during traditional holiday periods such as Thanksgiving and Christmas. The secret here is to have a comfortable holiday and not let anyone know you're back until your second day back at the office. Plan your vacation as you would plan any other project. Make room for contingencies and delegate authority to others. Work diligently to ensure your return to work is as stress-free as your vacation itself.

5

The Active Agenda: Demonstration and Communication

The Active Agenda is the figurehead for the section of *Cool Time and the Two-Pound Bucket* dedicated to communicating your time management abilities and negotiating through time and work conflicts. After all, time management tips and tricks are of little use if you cannot implement them into your work environment. Just as the two-pound bucket is an actual bucket, the Active Agenda itself represents a calendar, properly and thoroughly maintained. Rather than being a symbol of obsessive behavior, it is a tool, first for organization, but then — as described in the following mini-chapters — for demonstration and communication.

The Active Agenda Itself

Many people are already adept at keeping track of the things that must get done in their day, their week, and their month, but often this tracking is relegated to slips of paper, one or more appointment systems, and short-term memory. Some people prefer to use a traditional paper-based system, such as a leather-bound day planner, while others use calendaring software or handheld devices. It is of no matter which medium you choose, so long as it is comfortable and usable.

Many, however, do not make their calendar system as active as it should be, and utilizing it well is what this section is all about. Your Active Agenda should first and foremost be a singular authority. *All* of your tasks and appointments — both professional and personal — should exist together on one list, rather than scattered on napkins, sticky notes, or slips of paper. The Active Agenda should be centrally available, accessible, editable, and reliable wherever you go. It should be "active" in the truest sense of the word.

An "active" agenda should be edited many times a day to keep up with your changing schedule. Tasks are moved from the To-Do list to the day calendar, or from the day calendar back to the To-Do list, according to the activities and achievements of your day. Appointments are re-edited to reflect the correct start and end times, and to insert notes on events just finished. Appointments that didn't pan out are moved back onto the To-Do list, so that they aren't forgotten. Your Active Agenda echoes the principle of the project plan in classic project management. It is a living, breathing thing that will serve you throughout the day if you simply keep it well fed with up-to-date information.

Appointments and To-Do's

As you schedule your activities for today, tomorrow, and the rest of the year, they will generally fall into one of two categories:

- **Appointments**, for which you have to be at a pre-arranged place and time, usually to interact with other people. The defining feature of an appointment is its fixed starting time.
- **To-Do's**, which are usually tasks that have to be done at some time in the near future, but have no specific start or end time set. To-Do's are a major source of time wastage because they lack a defined time, which is what makes the Active Agenda process so useful.

Here is a sample day schedule, with I-Beam Reviews, a Keystone Period, and message-returning periods all scheduled. At the right is a typical To-Do list.

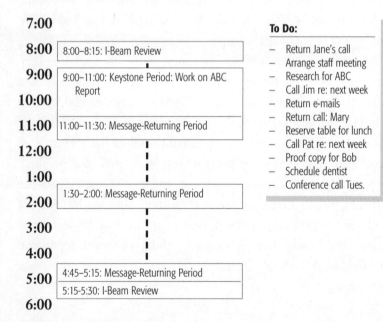

7:00		**To Do:**
8:00	8:00–8:15: I-Beam Review	– Return Jane's call
9:00	9:00–11:00: Keystone Period: Work on ABC Report	– Arrange staff meeting
10:00		– Research for ABC
11:00	11:00–11:30: Message-Returning Period	– Call Jim re: next week
12:00		– Return e-mails
1:00		– Return call: Mary
2:00	1:30–2:00: Message-Returning Period	– Reserve table for lunch
3:00		– Call Pat re: next week
4:00		– Proof copy for Bob
5:00	4:45–5:15: Message-Returning Period / 5:15-5:30: I-Beam Review	– Schedule dentist
6:00		– Conference call Tues.

124

The items on the To-Do list vary in terms of priority and content, but they have these three things in common:

1. None has a fixed start time.
2. None has a clearly defined duration.
3. Each will take some time to complete.

This is where many people slip up. When reviewing the day calendar, the To-Do's often remain timeless. Therefore, if there are ten To-Do's on the list, but the calendar day has no appointments scheduled, the mind quickly perceives that the day is pretty clear.

However, what if you were to say that each of the To-Do's listed above actually took 15 minutes to complete? If you were to schedule each one of those To-Do's as a fixed appointment in your calendar, they would add up to 150 minutes (two and a half hours), which would fill your day up pretty quickly. This may not be good news, especially if you have a number of other projects slated for your afternoon. But successful time management doesn't come from wishing: it comes from knowing that these To-Do's will actually take up time, and that you haven't got as much time available today as you think. It comes from using the morning I-Beam Review to *move* (hence the term "active") each of the To-Do activities physically down onto the day calendar to observe the possible usage of your time. This Active Agenda technique will help you reprioritize before the activities of the day start, enabling you to deflect, delegate, or simply say "No" to additional tasks, and allowing you to control the activities of your day.

In addition to giving you a hefty dose of reality at the start of the day, the Active Agenda technique can keep your calendar up-to-date at all times. Say, for example, using the calendar on page 124, you decide to assign "Proof copy for Bob" to your afternoon time slot. Be sure, then, to physically transfer the To-Do entitled "Proof copy for Bob" onto the calendar, rather than leaving it on the To-Do list. This may appear trivial at first glance, but it goes a long way toward making your calendar real, in terms of dealing with work overload, conflicts, and prioritization. Similarly, if a task scheduled for the afternoon gets preempted by a higher priority task, be sure to drag it back onto the To-Do list where it will roll over onto tomorrow's list.

These actions are most easily done with time management software, but pencil and eraser work equally well with a book-based calendar. The trick is to make the principle of Active Agenda revision a habit.

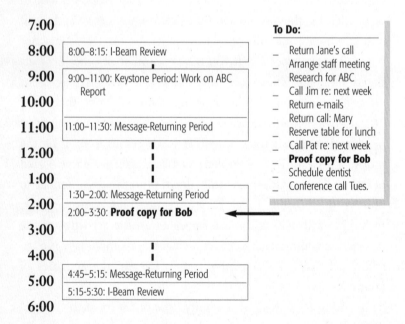

		To Do:
7:00		
8:00	8:00–8:15: I-Beam Review	_ Return Jane's call
		_ Arrange staff meeting
9:00	9:00–11:00: Keystone Period: Work on ABC Report	_ Research for ABC
10:00		_ Call Jim re: next week
		_ Return e-mails
11:00	11:00–11:30: Message-Returning Period	_ Return call: Mary
		_ Reserve table for lunch
12:00		_ Call Pat re: next week
		_ **Proof copy for Bob**
1:00		_ Schedule dentist
	1:30–2:00: Message-Returning Period	_ Conference call Tues.
2:00	2:00–3:30: **Proof copy for Bob**	
3:00		
4:00		
5:00	4:45–5:15: Message-Returning Period	
	5:15-5:30: I-Beam Review	
6:00		

Keep this Active Agenda with you at all times. Changes are more likely to be effective if you edit your single list immediately, rather than waiting until you return to the office and risking that you'll forget them in the process. If you carry a Personal Digital Assistant (PDA) or a day planner–style book, then take a moment to update it immediately before moving on.

All activities should be entered in the agenda, even those that you have no intention of actually doing today. The same applies for activities that are to start six months from now. Short-term memory is no match for long-term recording in an Active Agenda. Long-term activities will stay there and never "fall through the cracks." Schedule birthdays, anniversaries, recurring events, and all other upcoming events. Schedule them now while they're fresh in your mind. It's easy to forget a birthday or meeting, but it's very difficult explaining that to someone special later on.

Record activities, appointments, and events the moment you think of them. If you're not near your Active Agenda for some reason, write them where they will not get lost and update your agenda as soon as you can.

Beware of the yellow sticky note. They are good at marking pages in books, but they're ineffective as a reminder, as your eyes will become immune to them in no time.

Print your calendar once a month. If you use software for scheduling, make sure to make adequate backups, both on disk and on paper. As useful as computers are, they are still subject to the dangers of mechanical failure, fire, water, electromagnetic disturbances, and theft. Up-to-date paper copies of your most valuable documents are a necessary insurance policy.

Choose an active schedule system that's best for you. There are numerous sources available, including software, PDAs,

127

paper-based systems, and Internet-based systems. Choose the medium that works best with your schedule and personality, and stick with it.

Turn Plans into Controllable Reality

In addition to the purely practical aspects of maintaining an Active Agenda, there is the "reality" aspect, in which a written, printed calendar is able to meet incoming tasks at the door and serve as a foundation for your intelligent push-back, as well as negotiations with superiors, colleagues, and clients.

To believe something, we must be able to see it. It has to be committed to paper or screen. Plans that exist solely within your head are still achievable, but their boundaries become soft. It is much easier to lose control over a scheduled activity, to make it vulnerable to distraction and delay, when its description and timeline are visible only in your mind. To take control of any project, whether it is a diet, an exercise plan, or a task at work, you must commit it to physical reality. Put it down on paper and post it somewhere visible. Doing this commits it to your mind and body, and makes it real.

Furthermore, when plans are written down, it is much easier to make the necessary modifications as situations force change upon you. Your editable "living, breathing project plan" allows for flexibility, while not allowing you to lose sight of those tasks that you have deemed most important.

Day plans that are committed to paper or screen help you to avoid spur-of-the-moment decisions and seat-of-the-pants management by putting all actions and activities into perspective. They help keep everything relative when things go smoothly, and can be a savior in times of panic.

Recognize Your Achievements

Achievements on a day-to-day basis refer to every task you complete. They need not be as momentous as finishing a large project or getting a promotion. Anything that you complete during your day is an achievement, and should be recognized by crossing it off the To-Do list on your Active Agenda.

It feels good to be able to cross something off. Psychologically, it gives you a small boost, which helps keep the momentum of the day moving forward. This is why most day planners, whether paper-based or software-based, have space for either checking off or crossing off To-Do's. It is good to be able to recognize your achievements, to look back over previous days and observe what you have achieved. Crossing off your completed activities is a key component of the follow-through, allowing you to ensure an activity is sealed and completed before moving on.

Schedule Retroactively

If you come into your office at 11:00 a.m. after a one-hour meeting with a client, five phone calls on the road, and time spent writing ideas for your project over coffee at the coffee shop, make sure to follow through on all those activities before you continue on with the rest of your day by scheduling them into your Active Agenda — even though they've already happened. Schedule them in, then cross them off right away. Though this may seem like redundancy or a waste of time, in actual fact, you are recognizing and recording the achievements of the morning by making them real. You are following through on your actions. You are ensuring that follow-up activities are correctly scheduled, and you are keeping your diary complete by committing the record of these activities into history.

Sometime in the future you may need to review your activities for this day, and it will be a lot easier to account for the efforts and achievements of your day if you can see them right in front of you. By comparison, a big, blank block on your day timer from 9:00 to 11:00 is mute about your achievements, and our personal memories become hazy about such specifics as time goes by.

YES, BUT... As a busy professional, you may feel that such an obsession with maintaining a calendar is too time-consuming, and will result in days spent doing nothing *but* maintaining a calendar. I propose that it does the opposite. The time and effort saved in not having to search for lost documents, in not having to make up for meetings or phone calls that slipped your mind; the benefits derived from having thorough notes on your last meeting with a client; and the sheer comfort of traveling in Cool Time (see Chapter 8) are all dividends from the small investment required for maintaining an Active Agenda. Not everyone can do this, but when people exclaim, "There's got to be a better way," there usually is. And the Active Agenda is it.

The Active Agenda serves as the figurehead for the principles of demonstration and communication. Now let's look at how these principles can be applied constructively to your busy day.

Dealing with Conflicting Tasks

One of the biggest barriers to effective time management and one of the greatest sources of personal stress in the workplace comes from having to deal with more than one task at a time. They even have a name for it: *multitasking*. As mentioned in our discussion of the Keystone Period, multitasking is actually impossible, as our brains can focus only on one thing at a time.

Well, how, then, do we deal with conflicts? The first level of defense comes from a combination of the techniques we have seen thus far: assessing your workload using the I-Beam Review; using techniques such as the priority chart and the SMARTS test to single out the urgent, top-priority, and realistic tasks; and using the Active Agenda to schedule them pragmatically into your day calendar.

If you still find yourself staring down the barrel of a conflict, it's time to negotiate.

Negotiation is the art of achieving a win-win solution to an impasse. Its aim is to help both parties in a dispute achieve all or part of their goals, while allowing both sides to also save face. It is a fundamental principle of leadership and of dispute resolution. With regard to personal time management, negotiation is also a tool to ensure your time and efforts are used most effectively and in a healthy way.

If you're stuck with two conflicting tasks assigned by the same manager, then try to involve that person in the decision-making process. Ask him or her to help you identify which of the two projects must get done first. Asking for help in this manner is not dumb, nor does it show lack of initiative — in fact, it shows lots of initiative. You are involving the "requester" in the responsibility of moving other projects around and are seeking his or her help to ensure you perform the most important work: work that is of greatest value to the company.

Keep your Active Agenda clear and up-to-date. When people come to you with an additional task, let them see what you already have on your plate. They may not be aware of the other projects you are involved in, even if they themselves assigned these projects to you. A visible, tangible schedule of your day demonstrates your professionalism, your ability to plan, and your organizational skills, as well as your already-full schedule.

Make sure you are the right person for each of the tasks

assigned to you, and then assess their priority. Some tasks may not be for you to do — your time may be better spent elsewhere. Use the prioritization tools mentioned in Chapter 4 to recognize whether each task fits your parameters.

Approach negotiations with care and tact. Not all senior staff members or colleagues are blessed with the ability to perceive these time management techniques as useful. In all instances of negotiation, care must be taken to maintain a cool head and to not allow personality conflicts or politics to get in the way. A good manager should recognize the value of good staff, but this is not always the case. Effective delegation and positive relationships with team/staff members are hallmarks of leadership to which many managers and senior officials aspire. Take it carefully, and refer to Chapter 11, Emotional Bedrock, specifically the section entitled "Time Management and Senior Management" for further suggestions.

Saying No to Additional Tasks:
The Intelligent Push-Back

When a colleague or superior asks you or tells you to take on an additional task, it can be very hard to say "No." On a social level, it represents the rejection of another person's request, which can be awkward and difficult. On a professional level, it can also be seen as a career-limiting move, since displeasing the boss has never been high on the list of enviable employee traits. Some people can't say "No" for fear of appearing impolite, and to them, accepting additional requests seems a good way to avert a conflict.

However, avoiding saying "No" at the appropriate time is fraught with its own problems. It means you are working too hard on too many projects, and quality will suffer. It means you are accepting this additional workload, raising the bar of expectation in terms of quantity, not quality. In other words, people will constantly expect the same level of overwork from you. Most importantly, the additional workload condemns you to a life of working late and sacrificing your crucial non-work time, ensuring higher levels of stress and fatigue, increased risk of ill health, and a counterproductive distortion of work-life balance, as discussed in Chapter 7.

The effective time manager therefore must learn to redefine the word "no" so that it is no longer seen as a token of rejection or belligerence, but as a proactive, positive, intelligent demarcation of your abilities and planning skills — a push-back, a business deal. The word "no" is a line in the sand, not one that separates amicable working relationships from acrimonious ones, but one that defines the extent to which positive actions can occur. Beyond this line, tasks become more than you, as a professional, are able and willing to process efficiently. If someone is asking you to take on a task, that person is asking a question that has two possible answers, not just one. You have a right to answer honestly, standing on the Emotional Bedrock of efficient time management (see Chapter 11). It is up to the requester to be prepared for either a positive or a negative response.

Communicate clearly to yourself and to your requester that in saying "no" now, you are doing that person a favor. It's the "pay me now or pay me later" principle. You are giving the requester the opportunity of saving large amounts of time by looking for another resource now, rather than finding out later that the task cannot be finished on time.

It's difficult and scary to contemplate "pushing back" when things get to be too much, but there has to be a happy medium.

You, as a professional, have the right and the obligation to clearly demonstrate your current workloads and responsibilities as part of the negotiation process.

What if the Requester Is Superior to Me in Rank?

The reason you see the Active Agenda as the figurehead in this section is that it is a symbolic and practical tool of negotiation. Your manager may not be aware of all the tasks you have in front of you. You can help to prove your busyness by reviewing your calendar with your superior. Keep it handy, complete, and up-to-date. Help him or her to see things from your perspective. It's a powerful tool in the maintenance of your professional relationship and its resultant workload.

When the Boss Says, "Jump," I Say, "How High?"

YES. BUT... What happens when the working relationship between you and your superior is truly one where you are at his or her beck and call, with very little room for negotiation? There may not be any opportunity to negotiate workloads and to draw lines in the sand. Well, as with all the principles in this book, it becomes a balancing act, a decision that you, as a professional, have to make. Is the value of this "master-servant" relationship sufficient to justify the conditions? Step back and reflect on the Bird's-Eye View of your life and career plans (see Chapter 6). Where do you want this job to take you? Up through the ranks, to positions of greater autonomy or authority? Or would following this career path merely guarantee a position with a similar relationship?

We all have to serve someone. Even the CEO has a board of directors and shareholders who hold the reins. The point is, how happy does this job make you? How happy does it promise to make you? If you cannot answer this query quickly and positively, perhaps it's time to consider moving on. Seriously. You only have one time around in this life, and on a grand scale, time management is about making the most of every minute of every day of your life, because you won't get any of them back.

If you decide you must stay with this job and its beck-and-call relationship, then make sure to ask for a regular review of your job description and evaluations — not merely once a year, but more often than that, perhaps quarterly. Make sure that you and your manager are clear on your responsibilities and obligations. Don't let the workload drift into overload and obscurity. Stand firm on your Emotional Bedrock, which reminds you that it's right to be time-efficient, and you can only be so with clear, reasonable workloads and descriptions.

Making Your Time Management Abilities Known

Adopting some of the principles in this book may seem a little radical, especially in the context of typical corporate culture. Most people are simply too busy to take serious changes in behavior into consideration. But it is that very busyness that your proactive time management plans will help address.

Obtain buy-in. Demonstrate to your colleagues the usefulness of the Keystone Period, the I-Beam Review, and the Bird's-Eye View. Demonstrate to them that a period of focused work followed by a period for returning phone calls and e-mail is more productive than the current workday structure. Talk about the benefits of planning, prioritization, and balance. Illustrate that avoiding distractions actually leads to more free time and a more balanced life.

Get your colleagues to use time management. The principles in this book achieve even greater success when employed in a group setting. If your entire department could use Keystone

Periods, meeting plans, and project management techniques to run its activities, the sum total of productivity and employee satisfaction would rise significantly. Propose a pilot project of one month. Plan it as seriously and intently as you would a budgetary or hiring meeting. Work at it and stick with it.

Keep your tasks visible. An Active Agenda helps make your tasks and plans real, and helps others understand how busy you are. Therefore, make sure people can see that you're busy and well organized. Making your day schedule visible will make visitors less likely to distract you, and it will help you to avoid or deflect unrealistic amounts of work. Since it may not be physically possible for you to work in a closed-door office, out of sight, an Active Agenda helps you say, "Please keep away — as you can see, I'm busy."

Celebrate the successes of others. If colleagues employ all or some of the time management techniques available, make sure their successes are recognized by way of an e-mail or comment. Reinforce the positive feelings that time management can attain, and of course, communicate that to others. By making time management part of the corporate culture, you will be able to enjoy its benefits without feeling socially disruptive.

In sum, recognize the humble little agenda as more than a neat and tidy place to schedule your day. As a testament to your workload and your organizational skills it stands as a central pillar, enabling you to demonstrate and communicate your busyness. The skills of negotiation, prioritization, and delegation then take over. It helps you to ensure a balanced, manageable, logically structured schedule understood by the people you work with and for. In being active, it is really being proactive.

6

The Bird's-Eye View:
Perspective and Awareness

The Bird's-Eye View — literally, a high-level perspective of your entire situation — is by no means a new idea. In *The Art of War*, a manual of military strategy written by the Chinese general Sun Tzu more than 2,000 years ago, it is stated that every battle is won or lost before it is even started. The victorious commander understands and respects his enemy and becomes aware of the strengths and weaknesses of both sides, primarily by taking the higher ground, from which he can see the entire landscape, including his forces, the enemy's forces, and any other circumstances that may affect the outcome.

For us, the enemy is not really time itself, but our lack of control of our own activities within time. Many of us don't seek a higher vantage point from which to stop and observe the paths and obstacles that lie ahead. Is it any wonder that military strate-gists and traffic reporters alike both opt for this view? What better way to see around corners and develop tactics than to have the entire landscape spread out before you? So it should be for all of us, not just for the upcoming few days, and not even for the year. We must be able to take a Bird's-Eye View of our careers and our lives. You can't get where you're going when you can't see the way.

That is why the time management principles set forth in this book focus not just on the tasks that occupy your 9-to-5 exis-tence; time management success is derived from the thorough planning of all things that exist along the straight path of time upon which you travel.

Many people are condemned to endure wasted effort simply because they don't give themselves the chance to observe the larger picture of their own lives. It is possible to achieve your goals in all areas of life: career, education, family, vacations, hobbies, and so on; but attaining them requires the foresight that comes from planning. Some goals require energy and determination. Others simply require clear thinking. But all goals are attained more effi-ciently and produce greater results if they are planned for.

Therefore, as a complement to your twice-daily I-Beam Review, make sure, on a monthly or quarterly basis, to plan the larger phases of your life: your goals and intentions for the seasons and years to come. Perhaps you can assign this task to certain days of the year, such as New Year's Day and the two Sundays on which we reset our clocks in the spring and fall. Maybe you can get by with one Bird's-Eye View per year, or maybe you'll need one per season. But set yourself these dates. Mark them in your calendar and heed them. Respect their importance as the guideposts of your aspirations.

The Bird's-Eye View helps to give perspective to two major elements of our conscious lives: what is important, and what is achievable.

What is important to you? How can you know? Taking the Bird's-Eye View of a situation helps to reorder our activities and priorities and brings the "important" back into sharp focus. Some examples:

- **Staying late at the office.** You miss out on another meal with the family. You miss out on helping the kids with their homework, or socializing with friends, or getting exercise, or working on a hobby. Take a Bird's-Eye View and see yourself working away in that darkened office while the other parts of your life pass irretrievably by. Which would you rather be doing?
- **Handling crises.** Unwelcome events that throw everybody and everything for a loop introduce stress, chaos, and hardship. No matter what the crisis happens to be, from a fire to an unhappy customer, take a moment to gain perspective, to get a Bird's-Eye View, and to get a sense of what to do next before plunging headlong.
- **Succumbing to anger.** "Anger" is five-sixths of the word "danger," and for good reason. Anger makes us do irrational, hurtful, long-remembered, negative things. In periods of anger and frustration, remember to stop, breathe deeply, and count to ten. Few things done in anger can ever be repaired entirely. Take a Bird's-Eye View. Ask yourself whether the thing you are angry about, this infuriating thing that blinds you with rage, will really matter a year from now. Will you even remember it?

There are many times in life when we act or react quickly or without thought. These actions seem to resolve an immediate need, such as a backlog of work or a conflict of some sort. But time management needs reflection: it requires that we step back and regain an overview of our situation at all times. Strive to see the horizon and avert your glance, for a moment, from the immediate.

Framing Your Life's Project Plan

Again we turn to the principles of project management. As you use your Bird's-Eye View to identify those things that are important to you — both professionally and personally, short-term and long — start building a project plan.

Your plan will turn into a living, breathing thing, requiring changes and updates as time goes by. This is normal. No project can be run on an inflexible schedule. But a tangible plan serves as the central character in making your goals become real, and subsequent Bird's-Eye Views will help to steer your plan and your activities along a manageable path.

There are added benefits to be derived from actively planning your life. Your health, attitude, and sense of well-being are all heightened when your personal path is made clear. This elevated sense of well-being is then reflected in your demeanor, your mannerisms, your attitude. Some people call this charisma. It manifests itself as a glow, a brighter twinkle in your eye, the sense of comfort and self-satisfaction derived from the feeling of being aware and in control of your destiny.

In short, your personal project plan, in combination with regularly scheduled Bird's-Eye Views, guarantees that your actions and motivations always stay in focus. It is an antidote to the pressures and priorities of day-to-day life, which tend to render us blind to our true priorities through their sheer presence.

The following sections of the book seek to deliver a Bird's-Eye View of their own to help us understand why time management is so important as a life management tool, and why we as human beings seem to have so much trouble managing our time.

Putting Your Life "on the Line"

Time management, truth be told, is a misnomer. There is no way we can "manage" time in the sense of being able to exert an influence over it. There is no way we can make time act differently. We cannot manage time any more than we can manage gravity. On Earth at least, both time and gravity are fixed, constant, unchanging forces. Wherever you travel around the globe, you will still mark time according to a 24-hour clock, and gravity will still try to pull you down toward the center of the planet. What we can do, however, is manage ourselves within time. That is what time management is truly about: seeing how we work within the confines of the day and striving to make our personal performance better.

Our perception of time is marred by our culture. Everything about time is portrayed in rhythmic or circular patterns. Clocks repeat the same numbers every 12 hours. Tuesday comes around once a week, New Year's Day once a year, the Olympic Games every four years. Even the dynamics of speech are based on rhythm and repetition. They are the cultural echoes of our own circadian rhythms.

Circularity allows society to structure itself on predictability and standardization. It would be extremely difficult for any society to continue without it. But all that next Tuesday really has in common with this Tuesday is its name, nothing more. The great calendar-clock continues in its circle, repetitive and misleading, and we, as human beings, take comfort in that.

In reality, time is linear, not circular. Today will never come again. You can never return to a previous day, you cannot rewind time, nor can you borrow a certain amount of time from one day to use in the next.

Time is a passive nonentity. It does not do anything. It is merely the constant against which our actions are measured. Yet, as I discussed in Chapter 1, society fills its vernacular with phrases such as "Where did the day go?", which seem to make time a creature in and of itself.

The best way to break free of this elemental non sequitur is to start perceiving yourself in time's true context. Your mind and body together comprise a vessel that carries you along the straight — not circular — path of time. Take a moment to see yourself not as the person you've known all your life, but as a physical entity, a ship, setting a straight course into the future. And as you build this image, remember there is no turning around, no backing up, and no stopping. You are traveling ever forward. By the end of today, you will have traveled another 24 hours forward. Did you use that time wisely? Are you satisfied with your achievements? Were there moments of this day just past that brought you neither pleasure nor progress? Was time wasted performing a task that could have been done more quickly at a different hour of the day?

Remember, time management is about refining the way in which you use time, getting as much as you can into that two-pound bucket rather than simply settling for the most obvious "large bricks." It's about recognizing that a minute wasted in a bank machine line-up is time taken away from those things that you love the most. It's about turning the 80/20 principle back in your favor.

Money's No Object

What would you do if you never needed to work again? If money were no object, what would you like to spend your time doing? Take the time to think about that. As you build your awareness of your own actions within time, remember the things you love to do when you are not working. What are the activities that give you inner peace? Music, fishing, basketball, gardening, cooking — take note of the activities in your life that provide mental relaxation and give depth to your life. As you will see in the next chapter, a third of your day should be spent on non-work (leisure) activities. Though some of this non-work time may have to involve laundry, grocery shopping, and driving to various places, some of it must be given over to pleasure and mental relaxation. Reapply to these things the importance and status they deserve as key elements of your existence. Having justified them as such, plan actively to incorporate them into your day, week, and year as central components, not expendable luxuries.

Recognizing External Time Eaters

As we perform our allotted tasks from day to day, we find it's not as easy to get our work done as we might like. Distractions come at us from every direction, just begging for our attention. These things, which are the standard elements of a business day, have been accepted as a normal part of our corporate existence.

External time eaters are part of the corporate environment. They originate outside the realm of our own physical "selves," hence the term "external" (internal time eaters are covered in the next section). Some of them are essential to the smooth functioning of a business and cannot be eliminated. Some are unwelcome annoyances that cannot be avoided, and others merely provide a convenient distraction that helps to get us through the day. They all, however, take your mind and body away from productive tasks and redirect that energy elsewhere.

How many of the items on the list below can you identify as having occupied your time in the past day, week, and month? Can you add more to the list?

Note: This is not necessarily a list of things you should eliminate from your daily routine. Some of them you simply couldn't or shouldn't do without. For the moment, it's purely an exercise in being aware of the myriad actions that make up a day, listed in alphabetical order:

- (the) call of nature
- coffee breaks, cigarette breaks, or both
- commuting delays (traffic jams, transit stoppages)
- computer and network problems
- conversations
- (waiting for) elevators
- e-mail
- faxes
- fire drills
- installing software
- the Internet
- learning new software
- line-ups
- logging on to a computer network
- lunch

- meetings
- ordering supplies
- postal mail
- printer/copier jams
- telephone calls
- television
- trading stocks over the Internet
- training sessions
- unexpected special projects/requests
- visitors
- voice mail
- writing memos and documents

The point here is not to eliminate the time eaters on this list, but to be aware of their existence. There are 27 separate items listed. Perhaps you can add more. If you agree that two-thirds of them are distractions that happen to you on an average business day, with an average duration for each being 15 minutes, that becomes four and one-half hours (or one-half to one-third of a workday) given over to tasks and distractions that may be work-related, but are nonetheless taking time away from actual work.

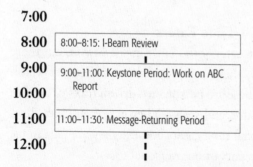

1:00	1:00–4:00: Distraction Items
2:00	
3:00	
4:00	
5:00	4:45–5:15: Message-Returning Period
	5:15–5:30: I-Beam Review
6:00	

That's a heck of a lot of time when you take all the time eaters and place them together as a single block. In fact, there isn't much time left to do anything, and that's precisely the reason for taking a Bird's-Eye View. When you step out of the rat race for a brief moment and actually see all the tasks that swallow up your time, it can be quite amazing. No wonder it's so hard to get things done.

Can you eliminate all these external time eaters? Should you? No, not all of them. But you cannot defeat an enemy until you understand it. Recognizing the sheer amount of a workday that is devoured by time eaters such as these is the first step toward refining your time management plan. Then the value of such concepts as the Keystone Period, the I-Beam Review, and the message-returning period will become even more apparent.

Recognizing Internal Time Eaters

Whereas external time eaters originate outside of you, out there in the working world, there are also time inefficiencies whose origins are internal. These are personality-driven traits or actions that cause delay, pressure, and stress. They are often more difficult to spot than external time eaters because they are part of us, the trees that make up part of our personal forest.

How many of the items on the list below can you identify as

having occupied your time in the past day, week, and month? Can you add more to the list?

You'll notice, by the way, that all of the time eaters listed here are dealt with elsewhere in this book:

- not saying "no" to additional tasks
- not delegating tasks
- attempting too much at once
- becoming immune to visual reminders such as yellow sticky notes or handwritten To-Do lists
- placing less productive activities before other, more productive activities
- starting on a job before all the facts or tools are available
- setting unrealistic estimates for job durations, completions, or deadlines
- not prioritizing activities
- not setting deadlines
- wanting to always appear available and accessible
- not tracking tasks through to their end (not following through)
- procrastinating
- getting distracted easily
- accommodating interruptions on the assumption that the intrusion is more important than the task at hand
- not listening or not hearing people's comments or instructions
- not taking notes
- socializing a little too much
- needing a break, yet working without adequate rest
- relying on a "system" that is all in your head

As difficult as they are to spot, internal time eaters are also more difficult to eliminate, because they are manifestations of your own personality. So much of what we do is simply done according to internal motivations: you refill the coffee machine because you're conscientious. You hold an elevator door because you're a nice person. Both of these are examples of actions that take time to do and eat into your day. Both of these actions are good actions. They each represent a small act of goodwill, and it would be nice if more people did things like that. But the point is, these actions are not factored into our perception of the time available for work in any given day. Few people will stop to calculate how long it takes to refill the coffee machine, but those minutes are being spent, not loaned. Our actions inspired from internal motivation come back to haunt us when day turns to night and we find ourselves still at the office.

So what's the solution? As I say at the beginning of this book, it starts with awareness. From awareness comes refinement.

Many times in my time management seminars, when I introduce the concept of the Keystone Period, or taking the door out of the "open-door" policy, there are always a few people for whom these techniques seem too radical, too novel, too unworkable. However, when we discuss external and internal time eaters and people essentially hold up a mirror to their own work practices, they start to see that time management need not come from an outside package. Indeed, a refinement of their own habits and methods is all they need to win back the minutes and hours that had previously remained invisible.

What Inefficient Time Management Is Doing to You

The two preceding sections describe external and internal sources of time delay. This section contains a list of feelings or impressions that people have told me they feel or have felt recently in their workplace. How many of these can you relate to?

- New tasks seem to arrive too quickly.
- Existing tasks are not completed before new tasks arrive.
- Things often tend to pile up.
- You can see things getting behind.
- Your inbox never empties.
- You are called to attend meetings even on the busiest days.
- You call others to attend meetings.
- People, phone calls, and other tasks distract you from your work.
- Your desk/office/workspace is cluttered with files, magazines, and other items.
- You have sticky notes on the walls, the PC monitor, or on the desk.
- You spend a lot of time dealing with voice mail, e-mails, and memos.
- You use phrases like "I'll get to that later," or "I'll get around to it eventually."
- You have activities and reminders written on scraps of paper.
- Your activities list is always too long.
- Your activities list contains tasks more than a week old.
- Monday seems to come around too quickly.

The items listed above outline characteristics that contribute to, or are a direct result of, inefficient time management. They are physical and mental symptoms of an uncontrolled tumble along the path of time. When humans experience a lack of control, they experience stress, which compounds the problem by opening the door to fatigue, illness, and further loss of control.

How many of the following have you experienced recently or are you experiencing right now?

- feeling stressed from work
- feeling a lack of control
- feeling overwhelmed
- experiencing conflicts between family and work
- experiencing fatigue, loss of sleep, or sleep trouble
- feeling resentment toward distractions in the office
- seeking out distractions or sources of procrastination
- feeling you are missing out on some part of your life
- feeling that you are seeing less and less of the people who are important to you
- feeling burned out
- experiencing lapses of memory
- taking work home often
- going into the office on weekends
- skipping social/family activities in order to catch up
- feeling anger toward slower drivers or slow elevators
- having no time for your hobbies or not having a hobby
- feeling out of shape and worrying about the resultant health effects
- experiencing "gym guilt" — saying "I really should get to the gym more often"
- having no time for reading books
- breaking your New Year's resolutions
- feeling like you'll never catch up

The stress brought on through feelings of a lack of control, guilt, overwork, increased pressure, and inefficient time management is a dangerous thing. It is important to get as good a grip as possible on the elements of the day in order to reduce the sources of stress and redirect your energies toward balance, health, happiness, and positive growth in both your personal and professional realms.

This freedom is why time management as a lifestyle choice is so important. It's not about being "neat and tidy and punctual" from 9 to 5 just for the sake of it. It's about health, wellness, balance, and enjoying things now, as well as planning for the future. As you can see, by stepping back and taking a Bird's-Eye View of yourself and the feelings you experience during your workday, it becomes clear that inefficient time management manifests itself physically upon your workspace and inside your self, to the detriment of both.

It is not always easy to eliminate the sources of stress in your life. However, perspective and awareness, goals and vision will help you to better deal with them, as well as to start devising habits and plans to reduce their occurrences in the future.

Remembering the 1939 World's Fair

If I were given the chance to travel back in time, one of the places I'd definitely visit would be the 1939 World's Fair in New York. It was a pivotal point in history, with the dark days of the depression just past, the clouds of war gathering over Europe, and — for North America at least — the prospect of a bright, gleaming, consumer-oriented, science-fueled century to come. It predicted a world of flying cars, robot servants, and technological wonderment. It promised that in the future (the 1980s and 1990s), machines would help us complete our day's work in two hours, leaving the rest of the day for leisure, shopping, and fun.

What happened?

In truth, the amount of work the average professional can complete in a workday today (even with distractions and meetings) would certainly be comparable to three or four days' worth of work by 1939 standards. We can do a day's work in two hours. But then we continue, and we keep on working until evening comes around, and everything we achieve or attempt to achieve still winds up being counted as one day's work. Technology has helped us progress, but our demands keep pace with the advancement like some form of ergonomic inflation. Though we're capable of jumping higher, the bar of minimum achievement keeps being raised. In the end, we still find ourselves struggling to keep up with our own standards.

Worse, leisure time often seems to vanish before our eyes, and work for many becomes all-encompassing. We have achieved one-half of the 1939 World's Fair dream: enough technology to make even complicated things happen globally and at the speed of light. But what technology cannot change is human nature. We work hard, we persevere, we survive. Extra tasks land on our desks and we doggedly take them on.

Cool Time and the Two-Pound Bucket is about changing that. Not by working to rule, not by causing disruption or conflict in the workplace, but by simply reestablishing a balance between work life and leisure life — a balance that was promised and predicted so many decades ago, and which we all deserve.

Your Perfect Day

When was the last time you had a "perfect day"? The kind where you sit back in your chair and reflect upon the day's activities with a sense of complete and utter satisfaction? A day where everything seemed to go right; a day that left you feeling relaxed and content? Picture the people, the scenery, the elements and achievements that went into it. Take a sensory snapshot of the feelings that such a day evokes, even in just thinking about it.

Those kinds of days don't seem to come around very often for many of us. We are too busy, too exhausted to even give this exercise much serious thought.

But this is one of the goals of effective time management: to recapture that feeling more often. Though you can't physically visit your "perfect day" location, or be with the people in your scenario as often as you'd like, you can strive to come as close as possible by re-injecting elements of control, self-determination, achievement, and satisfaction into every single day.

How do you do this? By taking back control. By using the Bird's-Eye View to see where you are and where you want to be; by using tools such as the Keystone Period and the message-returning period to guarantee you get the work done that you want and need to get done; by communicating and demonstrating to your colleagues and superiors that these techniques actually work, and that you are doing good work in good time; and finally by ensuring that every day is balanced between the three key sections: work, non-work, and sleep (see Chapter 7).

Your Perfect Workplace

In my seminars I conduct an exercise in which participants are divided up into teams and instructed to design their perfect workspace. Decisions on money, location, and hours are all up to them. The goal is simply to create the "perfect" environment for maximized employee satisfaction and productive work. After having performed this exercise hundreds of times with administrative staff, knowledge workers, and even lawyers and accountants, these are the responses, in descending order of popularity:

- The office would be located in Hawaii.
- Working hours would consist of a morning session of about three hours, then lunch, then a short afternoon session, ending at 3:30 p.m., or an afternoon session that would incorporate flex-time.
- Physical layout would consist of individual offices — not cubicles — with windows that open and doors that close.
- Staff would have the option to work from home, part or most of the time.
- There would be access to exercise and spa facilities.
- There would be on-site daycare and employees would have the right to go to the daycare at any time.
- There would be training and support in emerging technologies and trends.
- Greater focus would be placed on the communication of shared vision, goals for the company, and incentive plans.
- Management would demonstrate leadership and vision, and would assist actively in conflict resolution and career development.
- Computer systems and technologies would be up-to-date and standardized.

The fascinating thing about this list is the degree to which it focuses on "creature comforts." It proves that we crave those things that make us feel good, healthy, and alive. These points consistently emerged higher on the questionnaire response list than did the desire for better equipment or stock options.

Proof of the validity of, and rationale behind, the "creature comfort" wish list can be seen in the "perks" often given to corporate executives of a certain rank. Prizes such as the corner office, a convenient parking space, a door that actually closes, windows, natural light, office furniture made of fine woods and leathers, and an assistant to act as gatekeeper are powerful rewards, to say nothing of the generous financial benefits. Even newer-age executives who may eschew such highbrow tokens of privilege still invariably opt for casual, comfortable clothes and well-lit offices with nice decor. It's inevitable. These are all creature comforts: things that make us feel good on the inside. The fact that executives receive them as part of their compensation package is testament to their value to all of us as human beings.

The fact is, as soon as we get the choice, we go for the things that make us feel good.

You can use this fact as tangible proof of the importance of creature comforts to the working person. You can use it to legitimize and enforce a time management structure for yourself and your colleagues. If it were up to all of us, we would work in an environment very different from the one we actually do work in. And though we may not be able to change the environment, we can certainly make sure that creature comforts such as balance, nutrition, and reduction in stress are pursued and attained. After all, like the leather chairs and corner offices of our superiors, they contribute in subtle yet tangible ways to efficient, productive work.

The Work Patterns of the Average Human

Humans are social creatures, and as such we tend to invite and enjoy conversation, distraction, and mental stimulation. These things can be effective in enlivening the day and providing a brief moment of leisure, but they come with a price. For long after those moments of levity and distraction have passed, work remains to be done, forcing people to stay late, take work home, or make other sacrifices to get back up to speed.

As products of our Western education system, most people are usually trained in a skill and then enter the workforce, at which point their training continues through practical experience and further formalized instruction. We integrate into the corporate culture of the company, adopting the habits and norms of our peers. Focus is placed upon doing a "good job" and "pulling together as a team," while at the same time many of the latent, long-established time inefficiencies are passed on as part of the apprenticeship.

It takes us by surprise, therefore, when we learn for the first time that most people work at about one-third of their total effectiveness, meaning they actually will get only 2.7 hours of work done in an eight-hour day. Though this at first seems to be an affront to our ambitions, it does not refer to a lack of dedication or drive. As you have seen, the average eight-hour day is littered with productivity roadblocks such as meetings, e-mail, and drop-in visitors. Though these may be considered as part of the work for which we are being paid, a substantial amount of it — in combination with the consistent yet irregular order of its arrival — breaks up the momentum of work and stretches out uncompleted tasks beyond the sum total of the hours required to complete them. The difference between how much we think we've done and how much work has actually been achieved is surprising.

Classic project management, whose philosophy contributes significantly to the techniques in this book, states that when estimating the productivity of team members for a project or task, a project manager should plan for no more than two hours of productive work per person per day.

Two hours? Most people are surprised to learn that such a small fraction of each day can be counted as productive work in the purest sense of the word. And they would be justified in arguing that much of the corollary activities, such as meetings and phone calls, count as work. It's much like taking a stopwatch to an NFL football game. Over the course of a four-hour game, the ball is only in play for about 15 minutes! A good deal of the rest of the time is spent planning, reviewing, and resting. The ball-in-play action of the game makes up a very small segment of its entire span.

In addition, human beings work in phases. The body and mind ride a roller coaster of peaks and valleys, highs and lows, every 90 minutes. So not only are we constantly interrupted, but also our body, the vessel that carries us through time, oscillates to its own rhythm. We ride on crests of momentum and inspiration, then dip down into ebbs and troughs every hour and a half, during which cravings for stimulants — especially coffee or chocolate — make themselves very apparent. These highs and lows throughout the day, buffeted by changing blood sugars and ever-increasing levels of stress, result in a highly variable and unstable platform that we call our "selves."

What Is It with Chocolate?

Chocolate is a staple of the late-afternoon doldrums. Along with its obvious sugar content, it contains the stimulating alkaloids caffeine and theobromine, as well as phenylethylamine, which reacts with dopamine to release endorphins from the pleasure centre of the brain — the same endorphins that are released during periods of emotional pleasure, such as falling in love or making love.

As I discuss in Distractions (see Chapter 2), we are also buffeted constantly by the complications of our business day. Some are noticeable, while others are less so. The phone, for example, makes its presence known many times a day, but socially it is not considered a distraction, but a tool of business. An incoming phone call is a classic example of a "hidden" distraction. Many people simply take the act of answering the phone for granted, as something they must do. After all, who can resist a ringing phone?

But not only does a phone call demand your attention for the entire duration of the call, but once you hang up, it takes between six and 20 minutes for your mind to return completely to the degree of concentration it held before the call. That period involves a shifting of gears, a slow mental refocus, during which you are mentally processing and working at a sub-optimum level. When the next call comes in, the process starts all over again.

As if the distractions and the 90-minute cycles weren't enough, we humans have another impediment to efficiency: our built-in downward spiral. The peaks and valleys of our 90-minute cycles slowly creep lower as the day goes on. We are at our best, metabolically speaking, in the mornings, as adrenaline and light stimulus work to counteract the effects of the sleep hormones in our system.

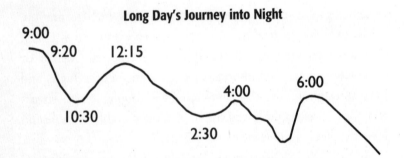

Long Day's Journey into Night

From that point on, the body slowly descends back toward sleep. In short, the first 20 minutes of any day are the most productive. For most of us, it goes downhill from there.

This fact is important to remember as you plan your day. What will you do with those first 20 minutes? Use them to work at your peak of productivity by scheduling your Keystone Period to start within this period? Or should you schedule a meeting, when almost everyone's cycles would be reasonably high? Or should you use this time to attend a lecture, to capitalize on your increased capacity to absorb information? How about planning to give a lecture or presentation, to ensure your audience stays alert? The choice, of course, is yours. For the time being, however, it's important just to be aware of the way in which our physical and mental selves oscillate across the spans of time.

A recent poll of North American professionals revealed that during the course of a workday, 25 percent of people's time is spent doing office work and attending meetings, 15 percent of the day is spent responding to e-mail and voice mail, 15 percent of the day is spent on the phone, 20 percent of the day is spent in face-to-face meetings and conversations, and 25 percent of the day is spent preparing for those meetings.

The fact that such a relatively small amount of the workday is spent doing actual work is often overlooked until such time as someone is called upon to make an estimate on the delivery date of a project. The effective time manager takes this small work window into consideration and calculates accordingly. We cannot do much to change our metabolism, or those of our colleagues, but we can do a lot to maintain our physical and mental selves through rest, nutrition, and exercise, and to capitalize on our understanding of how we, as humans, work.

Not only is this useful for individual projects, but imagine the positive effect it could have within a corporate workplace, in which all meetings, Keystone Periods, seminars, and breaks are structured to conform to human metabolic ebbs and flows. Achieving this would take some work. It would be on par with steering a large freighter through a strait in which heavy tides and shifting sands require constant vigilance. Given that this strait is the only possible route to take, it would be foolish to attempt the trip without someone at the helm. And that's what holds many companies, departments, and individuals back from attaining maximized productivity and satisfaction. Work habits become ingrained, and the ongoing corporate culture never has the time, money, or resources to locate someone to take the helm and navigate optimally.

The Circadian Rhythm Section

As I mentioned in the previous section, mornings are the period of highest energy and alertness for most people. Biologically, we are a light-loving species. Our minds and metabolisms react to the changes in light and dark, resulting in a complex ballet of hormones, enzymes, and secretions such as melatonin (thought to be instrumental in the production of sleep), serotonin (which inhibits sleep), and cortisol (produced during periods of stress). This daily rhythm, one of many rhythms to which the human body moves, is called *circadian*, from the Latin words *circa* (around) and *dies* (day).

However, most of us do not get enough sleep, which is why that morning coffee seems so essential: coffee helps move adrenaline into the blood supply for that extra morning boost. (Further discussion on sleep can be found in the next chapter.)

Other peoples' circadian rhythms gravitate to later hours, and they find their productivity and energy levels rise into the small hours of the morning. Certain individuals, for example, are able to rise effortlessly at 4:30 a.m., while others have more trouble. A number of tests have been conducted in which volunteers take temporary residence in laboratory rooms, or even subterranean caves, where there are no windows, no clocks, and no changes in lighting. When left to their own circadian rhythms, these people often gravitate toward a 26- to 30-hour day, in which uninterrupted work and sleep periods of over 13 hours each are recorded. Their patterns of sleep, food, and work fall into this longer structure without being noticed by the subjects themselves, who think they are working just a "regular" day.

Studies of cave explorers and deep-sea explorers have also shown periods of work, uninterrupted by sleep, lasting up to 36 hours. Devoid of the changes in light, the rhythms of the body are able to extend themselves imperceptibly.

To work better with your colleagues, an understanding of the effect of circadian rhythms helps in the pinpointing of optimum times for meetings, presentations, and other gatherings. Though you can never please all people all of the time, your decision about when to schedule your next major strategy meeting should be more than simply one of agenda-matching. Consciously aiming for that period in the day when most people are at their best, and consciously avoiding the time when they're guaranteed to be at their worst, ensures more successful meetings and more productive outcomes.

Workaholism

For some people, being called a workaholic is a compliment. They think it implies someone who works hard all the time, shoulder to the wheel, a real achiever. But though workaholics may aspire to those attributes, workaholism has more in common with the symptoms of alcoholism, in that the addictive activities go beyond the realm of the reasonable and turn inwards, becoming professionally and personally destructive.

Workaholics see nothing wrong with regularly doing the following:

- working into the evening
- working on weekends
- working on holidays
- working through lunch hours
- coming in on weekends to "clear up a few things"
- eating lunch at their desk
- eating too fast, then going straight back to work
- skipping meals, but still working
- putting off activities with family or friends in order to get work done

Let's make sure to set a distinction between working hard, working overtime, and workaholism. Working hard is the diligent application of our energies and talents into tasks that have been properly identified, prioritized, and scheduled, with minimal distraction or disruption. This is the kind of work that time management aspires to generate, since it allows for maximized productivity without upsetting a healthy work-life balance.

Working overtime means putting in a few more hours than we should once in a while. There are times when working overtime has its rewards: meeting a deadline on a "crunch" project, or making some extra cash for the holidays, for example. The healthy rule is that overtime remains infrequent, rather than the norm.

Workaholism can be defined as working overtime all the time, and often on the wrong things. Workaholics see themselves as dedicated team players and efficient professionals. However, many psychologists and work experts beg to differ. They point out that workaholism is actually a sign of inefficiency, poor work habits, and poor management habits, in which the attraction to minutiae and "work for the sake of work" outstrips productivity and progress. Most workaholics are not aware that they've crossed the boundary into inefficiency. Instead, they simply see themselves as relentless producers, focused on a distant goal that just needs a few more hours of work to complete.

Is this you? Do you work overtime chronically or just occasionally? Do you do it because you want to, because someone else says you have to, or because you say you have to? Is the work you do during your overtime worth it? Is the net result after taxes and after realizing what else you could have done with those hours still worth it? Is it interfering with other areas of your life, so that the deficiency becomes tangible? In other words, what are you sacrificing for the privilege of working overtime?

Take a moment to consider the work you do during overtime. What kind of work is it? If it is top-priority "real" work, then why aren't you doing it during the day? If you answer, "because there's no time available during the day," or "there are too many distractions," or "there's simply too much going on right now," then it's time to restructure your day and your week, as I discuss in the previous sections of this book (see Chapters 2 and 4).

If the work you're doing during overtime is not top priority, but "cleaning up, catching up, and just getting stuff done," then you truly are wading into the murky waters of workaholism. Many workaholics tend to lose sight of achieving specific results and fall victim to the need to simply "do things." For example, deciding to reorganize a filing cabinet on the spur of the moment, or resetting the typeface and layout of a report before having finished the first draft, may be considered minutiae-type distractions typical of workaholism.

In general, workaholics display actions and priorities inconsistent with true productivity. Workaholism is an addiction to work for work's sake. There is a tendency to gravitate toward time-consuming tasks and to work the longest hours on the least productive or least practical tasks, since workaholism is an addiction to work, not results. Workaholics tend to focus on tasks that are immediately visible, rather than establishing priority and then focusing on the top-ranked task. They avoid delegation, preferring to assign themselves to even the most minute element of a project.

If you find yourself working in this fashion, remember that time management isn't simply about getting things done. It's about getting them done in good time, to allow for a healthy work-life balance. There's only so much you can do in a 24-hour day and these "important but not priority" tasks need to be assigned time within daylight hours, which is possible as long as you plan correctly.

If you find yourself under pressure from a superior to chronically stay late to get your work done, this is not so much workaholism as an imbalance in the "master-servant" relationship. I discuss the importance of identifying this inequality as part of the Active Agenda technique in the previous chapter. If a superior consistently and constantly requires overtime from you, whether you are compensated for it financially or not, the problem of organization and time management exists on a level beyond merely yourself. It may be a situation in which your manager, and perhaps the entire department, is in need of organizational standardization. This delicate issue is addressed in the concept of Emotional Bedrock (see Chapter 11).

Technology Is a Tool, Not a Solution
The technologies we work with in our offices today certainly help us to accomplish a lot of things. What once took a week now takes minutes, and most of us would admit that it would be very diffi-

cult to go back to a world without computers, mobile phones, and fiber optics.

But these efficiencies come at a price. Daily, we encounter the downside to the mechanized world: computers, photocopiers, and networks are prone to mechanical disruption of some kind, and even when they're working properly, time and money are regularly spent on upgrades while the staff who are expected to use them are dispatched on training sessions.

If it takes you 15 minutes to send a fax because you are not familiar with your fax software, the productivity potential of that product is reduced to a point at which sending the fax the "old-fashioned way" would prove more time-effective. Once the software is mastered, however, its usefulness is realized and with repeated use, a dividend to the initial investment in time starts to appear. But until that level of expertise is attained, people and businesses are forced to work at a disadvantage. And this is the key problem: at this point in our history we find ourselves continually in a state of upgrade. We never get the chance to master our technologies before new ones appear. Our efficient use of time suffers due to an inefficient use of technology, which is itself caused by inadequate exposure to these products combined with a relentless onslaught of upgrades, replacements, and fixes.

Most people in the corporate world never get the chance to learn or use more than 10 or 20 percent of the potential of any piece of technology. Why? They never get the chance to practice what they've been taught, and they're too busy with other tasks to try to learn it on their own. They struggle on, grudgingly accepting the meager performance of their business technologies and doing the best they can.

A flip side to this technology problem lies in our ability to quickly accept upgrades as the new status quo. When a computer is replaced by one that has twice the chip speed, the first few hours on the new machine feel amazingly fast. But very soon the operator forgets the older machine and considers the speed of the existing PC to be the norm. The difference between the two machines would only be remembered if that person were asked to return to the older machine.

So technology once again loses in its bid to be fully appreciated by its user-public by being too readily accepted when it does work, and too quickly blamed when inexperienced people make it stop working. It becomes the scapegoat — sometimes deserving, sometimes less so — for many of our time management problems.

Furthermore, the ease with which we can send information such as e-mails and attachments has resulted in an "avalanche of the unnecessary." As Maureen Malanchuk writes in her book *Inforelief: Stay Afloat in the Infoflood*, we are not in a state of information overload so much as "non-information overload." People now dump information, in the form of memos, voice mail, and e-mail, rather than think their message through and communicate the key elements in a concise and clear way. The information also has a shorter and dangerously counterproductive shelf life. You may be CC'd on an e-mail today, only to be CC'd on an edited and updated e-mail tomorrow. The time spent checking the first e-mail in the worry that there may be something important in there for you was essentially wasted. Ambiguity takes the place of concrete communication. Copious amounts of "immature information" demand our attention and pull at our limited time.

The net total of the information revolution is progress, but it's not the pure progress hailed by pundits and advertisers. Business technology allows us to do far more than we could 20 or even ten years ago, but it remains necessary, in the interest of effective time management, to accept technology as a tool — a tool in need of refinement — and not as the absolute solution.

The proactive time manager needs to learn how to master the tools at hand in order to perform a task correctly in an efficient amount of time. He or she also needs to be able to separate the kernels of wisdom from the copious amounts of data that arrive daily, and be able to do so without distraction or delay. This still involves taking the time to learn enough about any given technology (from the humble photocopier to computer software) to be able to use it as an expert, as well as developing personal communication techniques such as writing time-efficient e-mail.

All of these aspects then return to the initial figurehead for this chapter: gaining perspective through a higher-level Bird's-Eye View. The intensity and focus of your work, an under-standing of your metabolism, keeping your office technologies and the messages that pass through them in correct perspective — these are the things that fill the landscape upon which your daily battles will be fought. Get to know them. Know them well.

7

The Balance Chart:
Work-Life Balance

As mentioned before, true time management does not constrain itself to the 9-to-5 working day. It applies throughout the entire 24-hour cycle, and is comprised of three reasonably equal-sized pieces:

These three pieces must stay in constant balance if you, as an ambitious professional and a living being, wish to succeed.

The slices of this "pie chart" are largely self-explanatory: the work slice represents the time you spend at work, doing the things you are paid to do; the sleep slice represents the time you spend asleep; and the non-work slice represents the time you spend doing anything else that is neither work nor sleep.

There are only three slices to this pie, and together they make up the whole of your daily working existence. For most of us, the slices are reasonably equal in size. The average North American workday, not including lunch or breaks, ranges between eight and ten hours. The average sleep period in North America is between six and eight hours, which leaves us roughly eight more hours to get everything else done. Weekends and holidays usually offer a different proportion, in which non-work and sleep dominate, with the work slice being nonexistent, or comparatively small.

The relationship between the sizes of these slices is one of the most important principles of time management — and for that matter, personal and professional development. For no matter how dedicated or ambitious you are — whether your career plans involve a quick rise to the top of the corporate ladder, an exciting trip into the world of self-employment, or simply finding happiness wherever fate takes you — none of this will happen properly if the proportions of this balance chart are not respected. Like the machinery that complements our modern life (cars, planes, computers), our physical and mental selves need maintenance to operate properly.

We need a transition phase to help us move from the mental and physical busyness of the day to a healthy block of sleep during the night. Incorporating a non-work (leisure) period into each 24-hour day helps ensure this necessary degree of mental and physical unwinding, which in turn primes us for a productive work slice the following day.

But for many people, this itself is just a dream. The pressures of our jobs force us to extend the work slice well into the zones reserved for non-work and sleep. Though we derive a temporary sense of achievement from burning the midnight oil, we do so at a great price. For the human metabolism is a strict creditor.

Sleep: Your Metabolic Body Shop

Did you know that the average North American adult requires ten hours of sleep a night? When was the last time you got that much sleep on a weeknight? Most people get six, seven, or maybe eight hours of sleep. That's why there are coffee shops on every corner. We have grown to accept caffeine as the balm for our fractured circadian rhythm.

But stimulants only help to alleviate the symptoms. Sleep deficiency is still sleep deficiency. If you get six hours of sleep on Monday night, then depending on your particular metabolism,

Tuesday starts with a sleep debt of two to four hours. If the same sleep pattern occurs on Tuesday night, then your sleep debt on Wednesday is four to eight hours. And that is assuming you get to sleep undisturbed! As the week wears on, the effects of ongoing sleep deficit compound themselves, resulting in sub-par performance, diminished attention, inability to concentrate, and a general reduction in productivity.

Though sleep appears to us to be nothing but a period of unconsciousness, the hours between midnight and 5:00 a.m. are actually a symphony of activity. This late-night deep-sleep period is the time at which our metabolisms and core temperatures are at their lowest ebb, our bodies are temporarily paralyzed, and we are effectively "shut down for repairs." This is a time of rebuilding, in which the body is hard at work replacing skin cells, repairing the minor damage of the day, reinforcing the immune system, and generally fixing the body up for its next shift.

At the same time, your brain constructs elaborate "what-if" scenarios, in which our sleeping bodies exist as both observer and participant. These weird dreams, culled and mixed equally from deep, long-held memories and the events of the past few hours, are splayed out like a watercolor in the short-term memory area of the brain. The thoughts and ideas processed during this time are, in most cases, forgotten when we wake up, which is why all but the most vivid dreams are hard to remember. In short, the sleep period is one of rebuilding, testing, and analysis — a nightly act of fine-tuning and adjustment that ensures optimum performance during our waking hours.

Non-Work: The Key to Successful Career Management

The non-work period of your day involves everything that is neither work nor sleep. Though essential life activities such as doing the laundry and the groceries are included in this area, it also, more importantly, includes relaxation, watching TV, physical exercise, hobbies, quality time with family and friends, dining, and all the other things you like to do.

No matter how ambitious and driven you are, no matter how much of a fast-track professional you wish to be, successful time management requires that you incorporate this non-work slice into your life. Balance, not overwork, is the key ingredient of achievement and prosperity. Here's why:

The mind is more creative when "released." Non-work time is a period of relaxation that drains stress and tension from the body, and allows the mind to roam free. Non-work activities can be vigorous, such as exercise; or they can be calm, such as quietly riding the train (even a crowded one) home — it doesn't matter. By letting or even forcing yourself to take in some leisure time, you will enhance your productivity. Ideas, inspiration, problem-solving, these are all elements that blossom when relaxation occurs. Carry a tape recorder or pen and paper to capture those great ideas, but above all give them the opportunity to come forth.

Having proper time to digest is central to weight control. A regularly scheduled non-work segment allows you to enjoy a healthy diet at a healthy time of day. Eating at 9:00 or 10:00 p.m. does not give the body sufficient opportunity to digest and process your meal before the sleep phase sets in. This results in improper digestion, leading to greater amounts of food energy being stored as fat. If that wasn't bad enough in and of itself, it also counters all the activity you might be investing at the health club — a double time-waster!

Non-work time invites healthy sleep. Like a boat slipping gently up to a dock, the non-work period of your day gradually winds down the momentum of the past 12 to 14 hours. It helps your metabolism gently lower itself, and spurs the release of those chemicals that cause drowsiness in preparation for sleep.

Non-work time helps you be your best. Top-notch achievers are always competent, confident, and capable. They inspire others, and are looked to for leadership and guidance. They derive part of this luster through some sort of non-work activity, to balance the stresses and demands of their work lives. By contrast, people who appear dragged-out, sleepy, and irritable seldom generate credibility or respect in the eyes of their clients and colleagues. The investment in non-work time, non-work activities, and healthy diet and sleep regimes can have as much to do with your success and satisfaction as your education, wardrobe, or experience.

You will gain prestige by managing time. There is a great deal of pride and panache in putting in a good day's work, then going home. Where, at one time, people looked upon the 16-hour-a-day workaholic as the go-getter, the company star, this trend is turning. If you need to stay until 10:00 p.m. to get your work done, what does that say about the way you run your company or your affairs? Excellence is derived from doing top-notch work in well-planned segments, rather than rafting through a continuum of never-ending tasks.

Whenever possible, consciously, actively, aggressively plan your time, ensuring equal access to the three slices of the balance chart. Sometimes circumstances impose themselves upon us, priorities dictate our schedules for us, and we are given no option but to modify our allocation of time to address immediate needs. That's fine. That's life. But those situations must stay the exception rather than the rule.

Most other times, you have more influence over your daily agenda than you know. When a meeting is being proposed, most people simply fill in the first available time slot on their calendar in order to appear available, willing, and dedicated. It's easy to say, "Great — put me in for the meeting" without reflecting on the implications of such a decision on your own agenda. The balance principle suggests instead that you consciously factor your three components into every day: a carefully planned work period surrounded by sufficient non-work leisure time, finished off with healthy sleep time.

Negative-Value Time

Given the absolute importance of the non-work period in your day, both from a metabolic and a career-based standpoint, there are very real consequences when you mess with it. When you perform work within the non-work period, that work quickly diminishes in value, and becomes a "negative number." Here's the math:

- **A** stands for the perceived value of the work achieved after 6:00 p.m. You could say to yourself, "I'm getting two-and-a-half hours' worth of work done this evening, which has a dollar value, or an achievement value of "**A**."
- **B** stands for the value of those non-work hours in terms of family, friends, and leisure. If you were to put a "price" on the time you spend doing things you love or being with people you love (or both), it would equal "**B**."

- **C** stands for time that was misspent during the day due to a lack of refinement, planning, and structure. Some or all of this time could have been given over to performing the A value work had the day been structured accordingly.
- **D** represents the positive benefits of the metabolic activities usually assigned to the non-work period, including exercise, eating a proper meal at the proper time, and the physical "wind-down" leading to restful, healthy sleep.

The formula, then, reads quite simply as:

$$A - (B + C + D) < 0$$

. . . and the work attains a negative value.

YES, BUT... At this point in a workshop, one participant usually shouts out, "Yes, but, I'm not there by choice. There's work that has to be done!" That may be true, but as I suggested in the previous section on workaholism, there are different kinds of work that you may think you have to get done, but in fact they can all be scheduled during your workday. They have to be, since they all make up part of your day and are part of your job.

Most people fall into the trap of not counting returning phone calls or finishing up some paperwork as part of their real job, viewing them more as "career dust bunnies" that exist but always get pushed aside in the interest of bigger things.

The efficient time manager recognizes that these items cannot be ignored, but neither should they be relegated to your personal non-work time. You can get everything done with careful planning and prioritization.

The balance chart shown earlier therefore stands as the figurehead for the concept of work-life balance, the Grail of efficient time management. But what can you do to ensure that balance remains a top priority in your life?

The following section gives you some suggestions.

Seeking and Applying Balance

Think of the definitions. Why is quality time called "quality time"? It implies spending time with loved ones or spending time doing things you love. Few people ever mention spending quality time at work. Why is work called "work"? It's an effort. Even if you're lucky enough to enjoy your job, it still consists of tasks, stresses, interaction with other people, and exertion.

Remember those things you love to do. Remember to plan them into your busy life — not a year from now, but right now. If your work is one of the things you love to do, congratulations! You are among the privileged few. People who love their work suffer less stress and tend to feel better for obvious reasons. But seek to indulge in something outside of work. At the very least, it's a good career move.

Opt for the Bird's-Eye View. At all times, keep the bigger picture in view. Where do you want to be ten years from now? What are you working on that's so important? Avoid getting lost in the day-to-day shuffle. Keep your horizon in sight.

Complete as much work as you can, then go home. There is no crime in leaving at 5:00 or 6:00 in the evening. The end result of a well-planned day means you have achieved your goals for the day, performed your most productive work during your Keystone Period, reviewed your day, and planned for the next two days. There will always be new mail arriving, always more voice mail to return. There may even be work left to finish. But you can do it at its appropriate time. Go home.

The Return of "Pay Me Now or Pay Me Later"

In Chapter 4, the concept of "pay me now or pay me later" is

The Marathon Runner at Work

Experienced marathon runners know better than to overextend themselves. Rather, they pace themselves throughout the race, reserving energy for the famous "walls," and ensuring they remain properly hydrated. No professional racer has ever sprinted the entire 26 miles, and no matter how lucrative (and short-lived) his or her running career may be, the true professional knows better than to run a second marathon the very next day.

introduced as a preemptive approach to time management, intended to demonstrate that marshaling sufficient time and resources up front is a lot easier than trying to play catch-up once things are underway and threatening to go off course.

The same thing applies to maintaining a work-life balance. In addition to guaranteeing that every day you spend on this planet includes relaxation, de-stressing, and healthy sleep, the balance principle also contributes to preemptive health management and career management, the ounce of prevention being better than the pound of cure.

People who work too hard for too long experience burnout, fatigue, and injury. Long-term illnesses borne from unrelieved stress do nothing to advance your reputation as an achiever. Your body simply can't keep up the same level of intensity for protracted periods. Thus, investing in even small amounts of leisure on a daily basis will contribute to the avoidance of longer-term injuries later on.

A Blueprint for Your Health

You can see by now that *Cool Time and the Two-Pound Bucket* isn't simply about working efficiently during the working hours of

9 to 5. It isn't about watching the clock while we're "on the clock." It's about how you conduct and protect yourself as you travel along the straight path of time. It's about recognizing that your body and mind together form your singular vessel of transit, and that daily maintenance is not a bad idea.

Air

If you work in a commercial building, chances are it is hermetically sealed. For the economic well-being of the building and its owners, the air we breathe is locked inside and recirculated. Revolving doors ensure that only a bare minimum of air is exchanged when people enter or exit the building. When you travel by plane, you get to experience the same situation in miniature. Dry, recirculated air is breathed in and out by the same people for hours on end. In both cases, in the sky and in your office, the results include fatigue, headaches, and a suppression of the immune system. In extreme cases, it's a contributor to "sick building syndrome," which in turn results in absenteeism, illness, and increased disability claims — an additional economic burden for the corporate and private taxpayer.

Can you combat this air problem by opening a window? In most downtown buildings you can't, but you can at least secure a more vibrant and healthy existence for yourself by ensuring your day contains at least two breaks, not counting lunch. These breaks are events in which you get up, leave what you're doing, and go outside. Even during the depths of winter or the extreme heat of summer, five minutes outside will help to revitalize you, forcing a badly needed change of air into your lungs and bloodstream.

If your office or working circumstances allow, you might also want to consider bringing in an ionizer and a small fan to ensure a flow of revitalized air around your face.

Natural Light

The human body thrives on natural light. It regulates our inner circadian rhythms, it stimulates us to get up in the morning, and a lack of it depresses our metabolism. It's no surprise, then, that the most coveted rooms in any building are on the outside corners. This is not simply because of the space and the view; it's light that helps us feel great, helps us feel alive. If you work where there is natural light nearby, you're very lucky. If you can open the window in your office, you're extremely lucky.

We need natural light. Many people in northern latitudes fall victim each January and February to seasonal affective disorder (SAD), a prolonged feeling of sadness, depression, and lethargy. The medical community pinpoints a number of sources, including the post-holiday-season anti-climax and the prolonged lack of light experienced during those winter months. We need natural light to feel up to par. If you do not have access to natural light at your workspace, you now have a second reason to take at least two breaks per day in which you get up, leave your desk, and find your way outside. Bear in mind also that you can purchase healthy desk lamps that provide full-spectrum light as an additional source.

Food

Try to get hold of the right kinds of food. Donuts provide a quick sugar high full of "empty calories," which, though tasty, do nothing to support your metabolism during the day and, in fact, counteract any good you may be doing by quickly replacing the "sugar high" with a "sugar hangover" that contributes to feelings of sluggishness and fatigue. More and more food courts and restaurants provide healthy offerings alongside the traditional fast-food outlets. They provide good, light meals, just when your body needs them, supplying energy for the afternoon and lessening the sedative effects of digestion, whereby blood is diverted from the brain and put to work in the intestines.

Eating healthy does not have to mean being boring. The physical desire for food, manifested in the brain as hunger, has been carefully studied by fast-food operations. As a result, their products are often high in sugar, sodium, starch, and saturated fat, which quickly satisfy hunger pangs without supplying long-term nutrition. Similarly, our craving for sweets, which from a metabolic standpoint is a cry for the natural sugars found in fruit, has been exploited by the dessert and confectionery industries — again at the expense of our waistlines and long-term health.

This is not an exhaustive book on nutrition, but time management must include maintaining an adequate diet. After all, it is the fuel for your body. You can't manage time without managing your physical self. Most people would never consider pouring a cupful of sugar into their car's gas tank during the next fill-up, but they don't think anything of doing the same to themselves.

The trick is to be aware of the situations around you and plan accordingly. Ice cream and fast food are guilty pleasures and should not be stricken from your existence if you enjoy them. But they should comprise only a small part of your overall proactive approach to food and nutrition. A meal that contains healthier elements, such as vegetables, grains, and natural sugars, will leave you feeling just as satisfied — and for longer — with less of the sluggishness that typifies the post-lunch doldrums.

Don't skip meals. The frequency of your meals has major implications on your time management abilities. Breakfast is the most important meal of the day (you've probably heard that before). Your body, starving after ten hours or more of not eating, needs carbohydrates, proteins, vitamins, and natural sugars to carry you through until the next refueling period at lunch. People who skip breakfast or lunch due to time constraints or an attempt to lose weight are doing themselves harm on both counts. If they skip because of time constraints, they are condemning themselves to perpetual substandard performance, reduced energy, and reduced attention span. Food fuels the body. Good, light food provides stamina. Sugary or packaged food tends to drain the body. Those who skip meals as part of a weight-loss plan are merely tricking their own bodies into thinking that a famine situation exists. When this is sensed, the body shifts into survival mode. As a result, the next time food appears, the body will store any extra energy as fat in case of another famine. So, skipping meals can be an effective weight-gain plan, not a weight-loss plan.

In both of the above cases, the solution is to aim for regular intake of reasonable foods. Have breakfast. Enjoy a mid-morning snack followed by lunch, a mid-afternoon snack, and then dinner. It's not impossible. Cheese, fruits, pita bread, and nuts are healthy products that need little preparation, can be stored without refrigeration, and are easily found at the supermarket. Five small meals a day will go much further in terms of stamina, ability, and weight control, but like so many other points in this book, it's culturally strange, which is why so few people do it.

Water

The experts say we should drink up to eight glasses of water a day. Sound impossible? Not with practice. In a couple of weeks, your body will get used to the additional intake of fluid and will use it very wisely. Not only does it assist in digesting food, it also helps balance the blood, clean out your internal organs, and metabolize fat. All while you sit at your desk!

Exercise

The physical benefits of exercise are obvious to most people. The body needs exercise to function properly — it thrives on it. But from a time-management and stress-management perspective, exercise also gives the mind a period of mental relaxation. Time spent exercising is actually time invested, as it allows for a mental break from the preoccupations of the day. The dividend comes in the form of clearer thinking, enhanced self-awareness, enhanced wellness, enhanced energy, greater stamina, and inspiration, as the mind revels in its new-found freedom.

Stress

Throughout this book I mention sources of stress and some possible solutions, both in the workplace and at home. Developing a blueprint for your health involves actively avoiding stress through planning, prioritizing, and having contingency plans at the ready. The effects of stress are still being discovered and analyzed, but its existence does not bode well for any of us. Working to avoid stress is a valuable investment in your future. Stress management is about controlling the spheres of influence around you. Control comes from time management, prioritization, and negotiation.

Work-life balance is truly that: balance. It is the fulcrum of success. Those who see "non-work" time as "slacking off" or "lacking commitment to the team" are not seeing the clockwise relationship of the three slices. Healthy non-work time begets healthy sleep, which begets top quality work, which allows satisfaction, which gives you license for healthy non-work time, and on it goes.

8

Cool Time: Perfection Through Precision

Cool Time is the heart of this book. It refers to the art and science of never breaking into a sweat, either mentally or physically, as you go about your day. Cool Time is both a state of mind and a mode of planning that focuses on excellence, as well as comfort.

Cool Time means that as you travel to an appointment, you do so at a normal pace. By allowing yourself sufficient travel time, you can walk leisurely and drive more safely. It allows you to enjoy a few moments of mental rest between appointments, to travel at a pace that guarantees punctuality, yet also allows your mind an unfettered period in which to focus on the upcoming activity.

Cool Time also refers to the concept of adequate planning —

taking into account contingencies, timelines, and constraints so that whatever happens, you are able to handle it and handle it well. In this fashion, the inevitable crises can be managed with your higher-level brain functions intact, ensuring a speedy and satisfactory resolution.

In short, Cool Time is about putting aside enough time to be truly "ready," and in so doing, recognizing that this is quite the opposite of wasted time. It's your investment in excellence.

Why is this so important? Quite simply, it's an edge. Most people just "get by." You see them running for buses or getting angrier and angrier while stuck in traffic. You see them eating their lunches at their desks. You see them buying headache and stomach remedies to counteract what stress is doing to their bodies. You see them counting down the days until Friday, when they can finally get some rest. You can encounter hundreds of instances daily in which people are just hanging on, no longer in control of their own lives. This is no way to live, and we have the power to change that by working in Cool Time.

People who work in Cool Time still have to deal with crises, managers, deadlines, and delays. But it is the manner in which they handle them that's different. Their relaxed, competent air is sometimes interpreted as charisma or leadership quality, that *je ne sais quoi* that some people seem to have and others lack. Their relaxed mannerisms and minds allow them self-expression punctuated by a brighter sparkle in the eyes, and the maintenance of direct eye contact. Their body language and posture are not bowed from fatigue. Their voices are clear and confident. (Stress often constricts the vocal cords, sending a clear message to your colleagues or clients that you are not at your best.) And as for visual appearance, Cool Time travelers give themselves the time to maintain complete control over their physical image.

Traveling in Cool Time

Wherever you travel and whomever you meet, your arrival is a statement about your personality. If you are meeting someone for the first time, you will have only one chance to make a first impression. If you are meeting someone with whom you have an ongoing relationship, then your reputation is on the line. Traveling in Cool Time means adding a few minutes to your schedule to ensure you present the best image possible to your audience. It can make all the difference in the world.

Suppose you have a meeting scheduled for 2:00 p.m. Cool Time demands that you eliminate from your mind the idea that the meeting starts at 2:00, and replace it with a slightly earlier time.

First, subtract ten minutes. Your arrival at the meeting should always be a few minutes early. This means that 1:50 is the new starting time. This will allow you to arrive at your destination with enough time to cool down, focus your thoughts, prepare your documents, and enter the meeting at your best.

Then, factor in sufficient travel time. Make a realistic calculation of the time you will need to get from your workspace to the meeting by 1:50. Is it a five-minute walk? A cross-town drive? Are there slow elevators or security check-ins to factor in? Accept these things as constraints (see Chapter 10) — don't wish them away or count on hitting every green light on your way to the meeting. Cool Time is about traveling without rushing, and includes safe, sane driving and stress-free movement.

Third, make these Cool Time elements real by entering them into your Active Agenda. Treat them as what they are: significant, tangible investments in your career, humble yet crucial building blocks of your personal success story.

7:00

8:00 | 8:00–8:15: I-Beam Review

9:00 | 9:00–11:00: Keystone Period: Work on ABC
Report

10:00

11:00 | 11:00–11:30: Message-Returning Period

12:00

1:00 | 12:30–1:00: Message-Returning Period
1:00–1:50: Cool Time Travel Time

2:00 | 1:50: Arrive for Meeting in Cool Time
2:00–3:30: Meeting

3:00

3:30–4:30: Follow-Through and Travel Time
4:00 | back to Office
4:45–5:15: Message-Returning Period

5:00 | 5:15-5:30: I-Beam Review

6:00

In this example of our day calendar, our I-Beam Review has allowed us to attend the 2:00 meeting in Cool Time. We still remain in touch with clients and colleagues via three message-returning periods, in addition to enjoying a full two-hour Keystone Period in the morning.

According to Cool Time, our meeting now actually "starts" at 1:00, not 2:00. We have expanded our definition of the meeting to comprise all of its support elements; namely, preparation time, travel time, arrival time, the meeting itself, follow-through time, and finally, travel time back to the office. At 1:00, as you get up from your desk to leave, if the phone rings, *don't answer*. Consider yourself officially gone. Avoid the temptation of answerholism! As of 1:00, you're already "in a meeting."

186

YES, BUT... What if the call coming in at 1:00 is top priority? Of course, as with all the suggestions in this book, it is up to you to make that final decision on what you do with your time. If you can identify through call display that taking time with this call is more important than traveling in Cool Time, then it is an educated, strategic decision on your part to take that call. If it is not that urgent, however, then let it go to voice mail. After all, if the caller had called a minute later, you would already be on your way and voice mail would take over anyway. As I discuss more fully in the section on answerholism in Chapter 2, resist the temptation to answer a ringing phone. As of 1:00, you're already gone.

When looking at a sample Cool Time plan such as the one on the previous page, many people react by suggesting that the "Cool Time Travel Time" between 1:00 and 1:50 could be better used in making another phone call, or getting a little more work done. The Cool Time principle suggests instead that one task done well is better than two tasks done half-well. If your I-Beam Review identifies this meeting as having a high priority, then the duration of the meeting deserves to be extended in your mind and on your Active Agenda so that it truly starts for you at 1:00. By attempting to squeeze in another call or task, you run the double risk of performing that task less well due to a tight deadline, and worse, having to rush to a meeting and risking arriving late and unprepared.

In the end, the decision is up to you. But here is a summary of the benefits of traveling to that meeting (or anywhere else) in Cool Time:

Most importantly, Cool Time allows you to be at your best, by staying mentally cool. There is an old adage that says, "It takes money to make money." This is also true as a strategy for success in the world of interpersonal relations. For example, the landmark book on negotiation, *Getting to Yes* by Roger Fisher and William Ury, details some excellent and timeless points on how to forge an agreement in which all parties feel they have won, from which further progress can be realized. It is one of many worthwhile books that can be used to help you achieve your goals as an ambitious professional. However, it takes cool to be cool. In situations of stress or embarrassment, it is often very difficult to find the internal fortitude and "togetherness" required to pull from the recesses of our intellect those key strategies outlined in *Getting to Yes*. When you are late or overly stressed, the higher-level, tactical areas of your mental faculties are sidelined in order to resolve the crisis at hand. Adrenaline supersedes strategy. Your education on the finer points of human and business management, those nuggets of information that stand to vault you to the higher echelons, will be unreachable just when you need them the most. Stress pushes away the ladder of success, leaving the key components undisturbed on the top shelf.

Thus, practicing Cool Time is not merely an exercise in punctuality for punctuality's sake. It is a shrewd tool of business, one that allows you to remain in command of yourself first and foremost, and subsequently to gain control of your surroundings and the people in them. You can stride into that meeting or interview with confidence, putting your best self forward. You will be able to focus on the right things to say. Your ability to strategize, calculate, think on your feet, prioritize, and impress will be front and center. No need for apologies or self-deprecating jokes. You can be at your best. You can think clearly. You can maintain clear eye contact and a strong, confident voice. You can remain in control.

Cool Time allows you to stay physically cool. Keeping cool is essential when wearing business clothes, and frustration can be a powerful internal source of body heat. A physically cool self means neat, clean clothes. It means a confident, dry handshake, clear eye contact, and a friendly face. Cool Time allows you to control your appearance. Before walking into the meeting, your travel plan provides an opportunity to locate a restroom and check your hair, teeth, wardrobe, and overall image. Remember, you have only 30 seconds to make a first impression, and you never get a second chance. Even when meeting people you've met before, a cool, perfect appearance strengthens your image, your credibility, and your personal power. Cool Time allows you a few minutes to ensure that you know exactly how you look. All of these items register consciously and subconsciously with the receiving party and serve to build their mental image of you, an image that lasts long after the meeting has concluded.

Cool Time allows you to stride into a meeting exactly on time. Lateness is abhorrent and largely inexcusable. It's disruptive, embarrassing, and professionally damaging to have to barge into a closed-door meeting, find a chair, unpack, and collect yourself under the bemused or reproachful stares of all others present. It is equally difficult to have to explain to a client why you are late for a planned and confirmed one-on-one meeting. With Cool Time, you arrive at your destination early, as mentioned above, with sufficient time to cool down and prepare your entrance.

But arriving early doesn't mean you have to "appear" until precisely the right moment. Let's say you arrive at a meeting a full half-hour early due to clear roads. Use the newly acquired downtime to make a few phone calls or do some work. With a cell phone, a PDA, and a briefcase, everyone should be able to continue with a certain portion of their work during unexpected downtimes. Better yet, you could spend the bonus time relaxing (imagine that!). Enjoy a few minutes of sunshine, read a newspaper, or grab a coffee. A 15-minute mini-vacation is a healthy, productive use of your time — it really is. Then, when you're ready, make your "appearance" five minutes before the arranged meeting time, exactly as planned. You will soon have people saying, "You know, I can set my watch by you, you're always on time," which is a currency that parlays into success very quickly in our time-conscious world.

Traveling in Cool Time also reduces stress. Traffic delays are inevitable, but if you have already factored them into your Cool Time travel plan, they become a little more tolerable and less wearing on the nerves.

Cool Time includes follow-through and return travel times. People often overlook the importance of following through, which is why it is discussed separately in Chapter 2. As you perform your I-Beam Review of the day, make sure to include sufficient time to write down notes or see to other follow-through activities pertaining to the meeting immediately following the event. Perhaps this can be done in the privacy of your car, but it should be done immediately. It must be considered part of the activity called the "meeting." The same thing applies to allowing sufficient travel time to get back to your workplace. Avoid the error of booking back-to-back meetings without travel time in between.

Cool Time gives you heightened confidence and stamina. By not letting small, avoidable crises such as traffic jams interfere with your mental equilibrium, you counteract stress and allow your mind to focus on truly productive things. Your demeanor and poise will be positive and dynamic. Your energies will be focused on progress rather than coping. The added health benefits of reducing stress in your day are obvious. A stress-free body has a greater chance at focusing on positive health maintenance.

Blood pressure, digestion, and the nervous system will all pay you back generously if they are given the chance to avoid being stressed during the workday.

Even if, at first glance, these extra Cool Time minutes appear overly generous and unrealistic, remember planning, not panic, leads to personal success.

Thus with Cool Time serving as the figurehead for the principles of "Perfection through Precision," here are a few other situations where it can be of great strategic use.

Cool Time in the Morning:
Mastering the Art of Getting Up

Most people hate getting up in the morning, and with good reason. The warmth, the comfort, the protection afforded by our beds is unmatched. It is a place where we feel most secure, even though we are physically at our most vulnerable. Have you noticed that when you travel, whether for business or pleasure, your entire perspective about the trip changes when you open the hotel room door and survey your new bed for the first time? This strange place is your temporary home, your private place of refuge in a strange land. In our minds, all of our physical journeys — to the office and back, grocery shopping, or traveling on vacation — can be drawn on a map as lines radiating from our pillow, the epicenter of our living existence. Wherever you go, in the back of your mind you will always have a plan of how to return to your pillow by the end of the day.

Getting up, therefore, is the first of a number of personal sacrifices and concessions that you have to make every day. It is a tormenting separation from the absolute bliss and warmth of sleep. To prolong the comfort as much as possible, a lot of people will run their mornings so as to spend the least amount of time necessary on dressing, eating, and traveling to work. And if they think of it they might even grab something to eat on their way out the door.

But getting up in the morning is one of the few things over which we, as individuals, have a lot of control. It is an exercise in mental determination: mind over mattress. Getting up in Cool Time is actually a recipe for success, achievement, and satisfaction.

Make Getting Up Worth It

Think for a moment back to your childhood, of Christmases or holidays past, of birthdays, the first day of school, a snowy morning, your wedding day, or the first day of a new job. Whichever of these you have experienced, you might recall that getting up on those days was probably a little easier than usual. There were big things afoot, things that snapped your mind into action and pulled you up to start the big day ahead. The secret to getting up on time on all those other days, in which big events aren't slated to happen, is to give them that same sense of importance. The benefits of being "up" must outweigh the benefits of being in bed. Your initial reflex as the first second of a waking day ticks by, when the alarm shatters the peace of early morning, must be one of action, not reaction. Rather than hitting your clock radio's snooze button with your forearm, move into a sitting position right away. Immediately start to think to yourself, "There is more to be gained from getting up now than from staying in bed."

Adapting this attitude may not be easy at first, but everyone can find something special to look forward to in every single day to use as currency for getting up.

- If you have a big event scheduled for today, a positive achievement that you know you can complete, then remember it! Picture it. Tell yourself that the road to that achievement starts right now.

- If you have a less positive event scheduled for today, something you dread, something that you'd rather not face, then focus on its completion. Look to it being over. Take the bull by the horns and tell yourself that by getting up now, you will be taking the first step toward completion and elimination of this unpleasant task, after which better things, or healing, can start.

- If your upcoming day and your job are mundane and you feel there's nothing to look forward to, then start by creating something to look forward to. If there is no satisfaction in your work, then focus on an activity or event after work that will make rising worthwhile. Sure, you have to go to work, but at the end of that workday is the event you've been waiting for. Getting up on time is the first step toward leaving work on time in order to get to your treasured event.

- If the weather is dark, rainy, or cold, use light right away. Turn your bedside light on as soon as the alarm rings, or if you have a partner who gets to go on sleeping, use a flashlight. Get your eyes and your brain stimulated by light immediately, and continue this in the kitchen and at the breakfast table. We are creatures who demand light and color, which is the reason so many people come down with seasonal affective disorder (SAD) during the winter months. Light and color before your eyes will work at eliminating sleepiness from the inside by playing on age-old instincts.

Don't Blame Yourself for Wanting to Stay Asleep

It helps to understand that the desire to stay asleep in the morning is a result of a built-in chemical conflict. The chemicals and enzymes that induce sleep are in conflict with those that are responsible for waking us up and stimulating our minds and bodies for the day ahead. As morning comes, assuming you've had a few hours of undisturbed sleep, your body lies heavy and relaxed, while the combined effects of cortisol, serotonin, adrenaline, and light attempt to pump you back into the living world. If you were able each night to enjoy the amount of sleep you actually deserve (between eight and ten hours), this imbalance would not occur, since the sleep hormones would dissipate naturally. But as we force ourselves to conform to the working world's clocks, we must fight this battle daily. The degree of achievement depends on your individual metabolism, combined with the aforementioned mental commitment.

Reap the Benefits

Getting up in Cool Time allows you to enjoy certain additional benefits, all of which contribute to your success as a professional and as an individual:

- **Starting the day stress-free.** By allowing yourself the time to rise, prepare, and eat in a leisurely fashion, you help minimize stress at the beginning of the day, which helps combat stress during the rest of the day. Though there is nothing that can prevent stressful things from happening during the day, a relaxed start keeps the body and mind on a level and productive course.
- **Traveling in Cool Time.** Dressing for and traveling to work with enough time allowed for the constraints of your morning, including preparing kids for school, walking the dog, and dealing with traffic jams or busy transit centers, allows you to arrive physically fresh, mentally relaxed, and on time.

Traffic jams and mass transit will always be annoying, but they can be much more tolerable when you know you have enough time to get to your destination.

- **Maintaining an edge.** People who stagger into work bleary-eyed, clutching a packaged breakfast bar and a coffee, are at a disadvantage and they know it. As they struggle to collect their thoughts and reorient themselves to the workday, you can already be off and running, working in your Keystone Period, or attending the other functions of the day.
- **Eating for success.** Breakfast is the most important meal of the day. Your body and mind are starving for nutrients first thing in the morning. A complete breakfast puts you in top form for the challenges of the day. In addition, reducing dependence on high-sugar, empty-calorie hunger-stoppers such as donuts will do great things for your waistline, which always feels terrific.

YES, BUT... "Okay," you say, "these points all sound wonderful, but I still can't get it all done. There's just not enough time to get me and my family up and out that completely." Actually, there is. After all, getting up is the first thing we do in the morning. We are completely in control of the "start time" of this activity, and can therefore build a successful morning, unimpeded. Here's how.

Redefine the term "absolutely necessary," and build that into your critical path.

As I mentioned at the beginning of this section, many people put off getting up until it's absolutely necessary, preferring to snatch just a few more minutes of half-sleep from the advancing morning. But in just the same way that we calculate our Cool Time meeting to include support elements such as travel time and follow-through, we can reconsider all the necessary elements that truly make a successful morning and plan backwards from our departure time to allow them all to happen. Calculate your critical path, your absolute minimum timeline, by re-identifying those elements that are absolutely necessary. (For a refresher on the critical path, see Chapter 4.) These elements should include the following:

- **Sufficient time to allow a cool, relaxed start to the day.** In North America, most heart attacks happen on a Monday. Why? The act of forcing yourself back into the rat race after a weekend is a physical shock that can have severe effects. Giving yourself time — enough time to rise and prepare without stress — is absolutely necessary.
- **A complete breakfast.** As mentioned above, sufficient fuel for the morning is absolutely necessary.
- **Time with the family.** Having enough time to help family members prepare for school or work, or simply having the time to talk in the morning without infringing on your own morning time, is crucial. Behind all successful time management and personal management philosophies is the importance of family. Taking the time to talk to your family in the morning is absolutely necessary.
- **Quiet time.** Allow yourself 20 minutes to read the newspaper or exercise. Really. Quiet time in the morning, before travel and before work, is absolutely necessary.

YES, BUT... At this point, many people shake their heads. There is no way, they state, that this can all be done in the morning. But there is. You have control over your alarm clock, and you have control over the time you go to bed at night. When you recognize that all of the actions listed above are necessary for efficient time management and a healthy lifestyle, you simply need to calculate backwards the amount of time required to attain all these things, and arrive at the critical path. That will be your new definition of "absolutely necessary."

Ultimately, you can make getting out of bed easier by reminding yourself that there is more to be gained from being up and enjoying a Cool Time morning than by staying in bed. Your personal goals, habits, and circumstances must play a deciding role in your Cool Time morning plan, of course, but the rewards will also be yours, and will extend around the clock.

Travel Twice, Journey Once

This is an adaptation of the carpenter's maxim, "measure twice, cut once," which in itself means, "plan carefully before action." A source of effective time management that is often overlooked is travel. People forget to factor travel time into their schedules, or if they do, they don't factor in enough. Trying to get across a city at 1:00 in the afternoon will be far more difficult than at 1:00 in the morning. One should never judge a trip in miles per hour (speed). It should be calculated instead in hours per mile (time).

People who miscalculate travel times are more prone to have accidents, since they're driving under stress. They're also more likely to experience road rage — a growing, and entirely avoidable, side effect of a population that feels pressed for time and no longer in control of its own actions.

Learn to live with the constraints of the road. Construction, traffic jams, accidents, other drivers, the capabilities of your car, the weather — these things are out there, regardless of where you are going. Expect them. Plan for them. Allow them to happen. There will also always be impudent drivers whose behavior is outrageous, selfish, and illegal. You cannot change the fact they are there. It's better and healthier to allow for them and plan around them.

Prepare a "Cool Time road plan." Though it may seem ridiculous to think "It'll take me an hour to get from A to B when B is only ten blocks away," a pessimistic guess that factors in the constraints of the road is a lot closer to reality than an optimistic hope. If all goes well and you arrive too early, you will have plenty of time to make phone calls, prepare for the meeting, or simply take in some leisure air before walking, in Cool Time, to the appointment. This also applies to air travel. Though arriving at an airport an hour before a flight time may seem, at first glance, an intrusion into your busy day, it can often be a blessing in disguise. With a laptop computer and a cell phone, or even a pen, paper, and a calling card, the airport departure lounge can be your private office away from the distractions of the workplace, a quiet spot in which good work can get done.

Factor in parking spaces and cross streets. In order to stick to your Cool Time plan of arriving ten minutes before the appointment, remember to include those annoying, stress-inducing factors such as searching for a parking space, checking your destination address for the nearest cross street, and anticipating delays due to obtaining security passes.

Don't sacrifice eating. Plan a quick meal into your travel plans. The fuel that the food provides will make you a far more productive and alert person when you arrive. Allow a few minutes of extra travel time to eat comfortably. It's as much an investment in your business success as the clothes you wear or the documents you write.

Enjoy the ride. Hey, a trip to a client's office is time you can't get back. Whether it's one hour or six, stress-free travel time is healthier and more productive than a nerves-on-end frantic dash. Let your travel time become a small pleasure in the middle of your day, rather than simply a means to an end.

Cool Time is about being physically and mentally at your best through planning, and about giving sufficient priority to those support elements of a task that make the difference between punctuality and lateness. The benefits of Cool Time extend well beyond your schedule and positively affect your appearance, your voice control, and your attitude toward the day. It is the minute-by-minute science of structured self-coordination.

9

The 60-Second Workspace: Organization

Stop for a moment and picture where you work. Picture in your mind the items on the desk surface and surrounding areas, and answer this challenge: Could you find any document in your workspace in less than 60 seconds?

Being able to locate any particular document in less than a minute reflects proactive time management, since every minute of your day should be used for constructive activities in all three sections of the work-life balance chart in Chapter 7. Your precious minutes should never be spent looking, searching, or shuffling through piles of documents, trying to remember where you left something.

For a lot of people, a clean workspace is the Grail that remains constantly out of reach. There's just never enough time to get started on a clean-up, and so the debris of the day accumulates.

Keeping and maintaining a 60-second workspace does not have to mean being obsessive about every minuscule detail. Nor does it imply that productive work should be sacrificed in the name of housekeeping. Instead, it refers to a degree of functionality in which any and every file can be accounted for in under a minute — which requires you to "put away" instead of "push aside." It creates a clear workspace free of distraction, which in turn reinforces a mindset free of distraction and ready for concentration.

There are three components to the basic 60-second workspace scenario: your physical documents, your digital documents, and a central index.

The principles of *Cool Time and the Two-Pound Bucket* suggest that any project or activity that takes your time and attention deserves to be uniquely identified with its own file number. Your company may already have a filing system with which you may wish to integrate, but a lot of organizations and small businesses have yet to formalize such a structure. The point here is that all activities that require some of your time and attention should each be given their own unique ID.

Assign each file a number and keep track of them all on a central index. This index can be maintained as a ledger in a book or as a computer spreadsheet. The specifics of the index are up to you, of course, but each file should certainly include a unique identifying number. If your office already has a numbered filing system, then these numbers should be incorporated into your index. However, personal files, such as one for all the documents relating to your house or car — or even files containing your bank statements — should be included, even if the physical files themselves are stored in your home rather than at the office. Remember, this is your personal index, and the point of it is to make every activity or project, with its support documents, easily accessible.

The nice thing about maintaining your file index in a computer spreadsheet, by the way, is that it is much easier to sort by any criteria: date of entry, status, date of last comment, file name, file number, etc. Also, by placing a shortcut icon on your desktop, you can gain instant access to your computerized ledger. Your spreadsheet-based file index can even be transported between your office and your home office if necessary, either by placing it on a floppy disk, printing it out, e-mailing it to yourself, or storing it in a PDA.

Assign each file a folder in your filing cabinet. This point is obvious, but not everybody takes the time to adopt it. This results in piles of paper lying around and the inevitable search for the lost document. The tedious act of filing documents should not be considered an exercise in officiousness and bureaucracy. Rather, consider it a part of your follow-through, an essential time management tool. If your filing room is not physically nearby, create a stack of "to be filed" files, and factor some time, either yours or an assistant's, to re-file once a day. Don't let the pile grow.

Assign a corresponding file folder on your computer. Many people do not exploit their personal computer's capacity to create file folders on the hard drive or network drives to the fullest. These drives are storage systems, just like filing cabinets in the real world. They are designed to be divided into subsections that match your needs. Few people would want to buy a four-foot-tall filing cabinet that has only one four-foot-tall drawer. Imagine trying to pull that drawer open in the hopes of ferreting through a three-foot-high stack of documents that have accumulated purely in the order in which they were thrown. Imagine trying to do that ten or 20 times a day! But that's what a lot of people do when saving documents on their computer.

Create folders on your hard drive or network drive that correspond to the file numbers in your index, and make a habit of saving your documents to them. Doing this ensures that electronic documents relating to each file are stored appropriately, and more importantly, can be found with ease.

The 60-second workspace concept, in which any document can be found in under a minute, is the figurehead of this section, which focuses on organization. The rest of this chapter therefore offers a few other time-efficient organizational techniques.

Cool Time Checklists

Have you ever found yourself already "on the road" when you suddenly realize you've left something behind? Or you think, "Did I turn off the stove?" or "Did I lock the door?" Immediately your mind and body go into crisis mode as you work to figure out how best to resolve the situation. Your heart starts pounding, you rapidly try to plan your next course of action, and your stress level rises. Often, your mind will also put aside a little time and energy to reprimand itself for such a silly mistake.

The things we do day in and day out become habit after a

P.T. Barnum and Napoleon

P.T. Barnum's circus in the 1800s was a model of efficiency. He was able to move hundreds of people and animals as well as hundreds of tons of equipment all over the United States, mostly by train.

The logistics of doing this profitably and efficiently were so great that Napoleon III actually sent some of his generals over to learn, in the hope that his armies could do the same.

while. But even so, the keeper of these habits — our long-term memory — can become distracted just long enough to let one item fall through the cracks. The stress of hurrying to get "out the door," especially if we're already late, often inhibits our higher-level brain functions, and complete memory is one of the first casualties.

By employing checklists for tedious activities such as packing, traveling, preparing for a meeting, and so on, you are doing yourself two favors. First, you are assuring yourself that all arrangements have been confirmed and everything you need is with you. Second, you avoid the stress and guilt experienced when the missing element is remembered for the first time. Third, your checklist can be edited and refined after each trip, making it even more useful as time goes by.

The efficient manager of time therefore recognizes the power of formalized checklists. Checklists relieve the mind of the need for perfect recall of mundane items. They act as a second memory. Just as a computerized file index keeps track of the topics of your life, so checklists should actively be used to complement and support the mental tasks that sometimes fail us. As well as keeping us from forgetting things when we are rushed or pressured, they also ensure consistency of actions, reduce delay, and help eliminate stress. Checklists for emergency or crisis situations can also save lives.

Here are just a few of the scenarios in which checklists should be created and used:

- when leaving for the office in the morning
- when visiting a new client
- when going for a job interview
- when giving a presentation

- when meeting someone for lunch
- during emergency procedures at the office
- during emergency procedures at home

Basically, any situation in which a sequence of activities must be followed and where a chance for mental distraction exists justifies a Cool Time checklist.

Invest the time to create checklists that address all the scenarios in which one might be needed. Create them, print them, and have them nearby: stick the list to your hallway mirror, inside your briefcase, on your PDA, or behind your car's sun visor. The principle is that this list should be checked and each item fully accounted for before the trip begins. If you use these lists and keep them handy, you will never leave things behind again.

For example, a pre-departure Cool Time checklist for your daily trip to the office may consist of the following:

✓ Calendar or active agenda	✓ Documents
✓ Cell phone	✓ Personal accessories: belt, earrings,
✓ Briefcase	tie clip, watch
✓ Keys	✓ Wallet/purse
✓ Am I presentable? (zippers fastened,	✓ Pen
tie perfect, hair perfect)	✓ Pager
✓ Business cards	

Your list will be personal and will belong only to you. If you repeat it every day as a countdown before the daily departure, you will quickly have it committed to memory.

Checklists are also extremely useful when packing for business travel, or when packing a road show to give a presentation to a client. The point is to list all the elements — the obvious things that you need to pack — as well as items or activities you have learned from experience, and put them together in one foolproof and continually upgradable "project plan for travel."

A Sample Trip Checklist

✓ What is the destination address?

✓ What is the name of the nearest cross street?

✓ Are there any one-way streets?

✓ Is parking available? If so, where?

✓ What is the contact's name?

✓ What is the contact's phone number?

✓ Is there an alternate contact?

✓ What is the alternate contact's phone number?

✓ Are there prior security or access arrangements to be made?

✓ Have I called to confirm the appointment two days prior?

✓ How can the contact reach me if there is an emergency or change of plan?

✓ Have I packed everything I need to take? (Add your packing checklist here.)

Precedent Checklists

Precedents are lists of related activities that stretch backwards through time from the due date. These are in contrast to the Cool Time checklists above, which are closer together and focus more on packing and going. If you can identify tasks that together form a pattern of activity leading to an end goal, and if you foresee that this pattern will have to be repeated at a later date for a related or separate project, it is wise to record that pattern of activities as a "precedent checklist." A simple example to illustrate the point would be in our earlier example of putting together a presentation:

– seven business days prior	Add custom slides to presentation.
– five business days prior	Send slide show to printers for creation of color overheads.
– three business days prior	Confirm appointment date and time.
– three business days prior	Confirm address, nearest cross street, and parking facilities.
– two business days prior	Print, collate, and staple handouts.
– two business days prior	Pick up slide-show overheads from printers.
– one business day prior	Rehearse presentation.
– one business day prior	Prepare and pack materials using packing checklist.
– one business day prior	Pack overheads.
– **Presentation Day**	
– one business day post	Presentation postmortem with sales team.
– two business days post	Prepare and send thank-you note.
– six business days post	One-week follow-up call.

Naturally, the specifics of your precedent checklists will differ. You may want to create numerous precedent checklists to deal with the various procedures in your professional and personal lives. What stays the same, however, is the value of entering consecutive, time-sensitive tasks into your Active Agenda. By doing this, you are practicing preemptive time management, saving time and effort by ensuring all the components of a major activity are taken care of.

The moment the word is given that the activity is a "go," the precedent list items should be entered at their appropriate dates prior to or following the event. This is smart project planning in action.

Recording Everything

How often have you said to yourself, "I'll get to it later," or "I must remember to do that," only to have it slip away? How often have you been introduced to somebody, only to forget the person's name ten seconds later?

Generally, the human mind is a remarkable instrument and has a phenomenal capacity for remembering distinct patterns and events for long periods of time. Smaller, temporary items, however, those that exist solely in the short-term memory area of the brain, sometimes do not get the chance to stick. In addition, it has been proven that human short-term memory can manage a maximum of only seven items at a time. Therefore, if you find yourself with more than seven tasks to perform today, or seven items to buy at a store, you will most likely forget a few unless you write them down.

In short, we can all do with some help in the area of short-term memory, and when this helps to keep items such as names, appointments, or tasks from slipping through the cracks, it becomes an important time management tool.

Make the act of recording data into your Active Agenda a top priority. As you have already seen, planning your day actively is central to time management success. Therefore, nothing can be more important at the beginning and end of each day than maintaining your To-Do list and your Active Agenda. Furthermore, as activities happen, as tasks get done, or as things get rescheduled or reprioritized, update your To-Do list immediately. Such attention to detail is neither neurotic nor obsessive nor a waste of time. It represents maintenance of your project plan for your professional and personal life. Don't let any day start or end without giving it proper care and attention.

Note down new activities and thoughts the moment you think of them. Whether you use a PDA, a voice recorder, or a piece of paper, get your thoughts and ideas down in one singular location for processing during your I-Beam Review. You wouldn't expect a physician to keep a day's worth of patient notes and prescriptions in the back of his or her head until the end of the day, would you? If you haven't got a pen, but you have access to a phone, call and leave yourself a message. If you do not have access to any sort of recording device, then try focusing on an object in your home or office. It could be a picture, a coffee pot, or a door handle. Visualize it. Give it a disproportionate amount of importance in your mind. Focus on that object, and make it stand out from the rest of the items in the room. Then, using word association tricks described in the next section, connect your idea to that object. Anchor your thought to that object in your mind's eye, so that when you return to your office or room, the object itself will trigger the memory and make it available for proper recording. Count on the fact that if you carry something loosely in the back of your mind, you'll drop it.

Use follow-up reminders, even for activities that are to start a year from now. No activity is too far away to be ignored. If it concerns you, then it should be in your Active Agenda. Whether you use software or a paper-based system, it should be quite easy to flip forward in order to note activities for future months and years. If need be, use a single sheet of notepaper at the back of your Active Agenda to list all activities that are tentatively scheduled a long way off.

Keep hard copies of important items. As much as the concept of the "paperless office" has been predicted and heralded over the past two decades, the fact is that nothing is as secure as hard copy. The efficient time manager keeps the important stuff, including printouts of incoming and outgoing e-mails as well as notes from the central call log (see "Receiving Phone Calls," Chapter 3), on file. Take full advantage of the techniques of the 60-second workspace to keep these files organized, neat, and eminently retrievable. Though this may represent a small step backward from the goal of the "paperless office," it is a major leap forward in efficient time management, reducing the number of minutes spent searching and improving your abilities to stay totally informed and on top of every situation.

Using Word Association

If you are confronted with a situation in which you cannot stop to write down a list of items, but must memorize them, use word association to link each item to an image. This technique requires imagination and quick thinking, but works very well for up to ten items. Quite simply, each item that needs to be memorized is mentally attached to a numbered rhyme. Though this may appear childish at first glance, it is truly an excellent trick for fast memorization. The rhyme scheme is as follows:

One is the sun
Two is a shoe
Three is a tree
Four is a door
Five is a hive

Six is sticks
Seven is Heaven
Eight is a gate
Nine is a pine
Ten is a pen

Assume now that you are meeting with the president of your company. The conversation triggers in your mind a few things that will have to get done later today, including the following:

- booking plane tickets for an upcoming business trip
- scheduling a lunch meeting
- downloading the annual report from a client's Web site
- finalizing your mini-presentation for tomorrow's meeting
- ordering a new suit
- scheduling a dental appointment
- picking up milk on the way home
- learning the names of the president's spouse and kids for the next time you meet
- signing up for the seminar being held next week
- booking a boardroom for the project planning session next Monday

Whew! You can't slip away to write these things into your Active Agenda, and worse, as you struggle to commit these tasks to memory, another senior member of management comes up, shakes your hand, and also starts chatting with you. The distraction that this second person creates will cause your list of tasks to evaporate into thin air unless you tie them down first in the form of the rhyming list, as follows:

ONE IS THE SUN

Goal: Book your plane tickets.

Association: Most people book plane tickets when going on holiday to a sunny locale.

Key image: Sun/holiday travel

Key thought: Plane . . . plane tickets

TWO IS A SHOE

Goal: Schedule a lunch meeting.

Association: Picture people at a restaurant – white tablecloths, lots of shiny shoes peeking out from under the tablecloths. You think to yourself, "Make sure the waiter doesn't trip over my shoes."

Key image: Shoes in a restaurant setting

Key thought: Restaurant . . . make lunch reservations, schedule lunch meeting

THREE IS A TREE

Goal: Download the annual report from a client's Web site.

Association: Annual reports use lots of paper. Paper comes from trees. Also follow the image of tree from the leaves, down the trunk to the roots. This symbolizes downloading from their network to yours – also, the fruit of their labors drops down to you.

Key image: Tree/paper/branches to root or fruit falling toward you

Key thought: Paper document to come toward you from the source . . . download annual report

FOUR IS A DOOR

Goal: Finalize your mini-presentation for tomorrow's meeting.

Association: A door and a boardroom table are both long, flat pieces of wood.

Key image: You sitting at boardroom table

Key thought: You at the meeting . . . is the presentation ready?

FIVE IS A HIVE

Goal: Go to the tailor's to order a new suit.

Association: Tailors use yellow and black tape measures. Bees are yellow and black. Tailors tend to "buzz" around you, making measurements.

Key image: Bees in hive, tape measure, and tailor

Key thought: Go to tailor's for a new suit

SIX IS STICKS

Goal: Schedule a dental appointment.

Association: Dentists use lots of strange-looking tools – they look like sticks.

Key image: Dentist's tools as sticks

Key thought: Dentist's tools . . . schedule a dental appointment.

SEVEN IS HEAVEN

Goal: Pick up milk on the way home.

Association: White clouds = heaven

Key image: White clouds = white milk

Key thought: Pick up milk on the way home.

EIGHT IS A GATE

Goal: Learn the names of the president's spouse and kids.

Association: The president is your gate toward promotion.

Key image: A gate = the president

Key thought: Learn the names of the president's family.

NINE IS A PINE

Goal: Sign up for the seminar being held next week.

Association: A pen has the same shape as a pine tree – it also represents growth of knowledge.

Key image: Pen/pine tree shape

Key thought: Need to sign up for the seminar

TEN IS A PEN

Goal: Book a boardroom for the project planning session next Monday.

Association: In boardrooms, we often use colored markers on the whiteboard.

Key image: Pen/whiteboard marker pen

Key thought: Whiteboard marker pen . . . boardroom . . . book a boardroom for next week

As you can see from this list, the associations depend on your own imagination. They can be as silly or outlandish as you wish, because no one else will see or hear them. The idea is to keep those key items locked in your short-term memory until such time as you can commit them to your Active Agenda. With practice, you will give your short-term memory a talent that few people have — the ability to accurately retain a complex list accurately and completely.

How to Memorize People's Names

Word association can also be applied to learning and remembering people's names. For many of us, the actions involved during a formal introduction require so much presence of mind (the handshake, the smile, the posture, the formalities involved in meeting), that the person's name goes skipping off the surface of our short-term memory like a pebble on a lake.

The trick here is to change your approach from mentally passive to mentally aggressive. As you extend your hand for a handshake, use the action of extending your hand as a call to action, a reminder to yourself that memorization must now occur. This requires no change in your outward behavior, no need to shake hands more aggressively. Simply, it sets the stage for the crucial next few seconds of social interaction.

Next, make sure you hear the person's name. Use the person's name in your response, as in, "Pat, it's a pleasure to meet you." If you didn't hear the name correctly, or if it's an unusual name, ask to have it repeated or try repeating it yourself. "I'm sorry — Pat was it, or Pete?" There's nothing wrong with doing this. In fact, it's a mark of respect, demonstrating to the other person that you truly do care about meeting him or her — a message that not everybody conveys in social situations.

Once you hear the person's name, use mental association immediately to tie the name to an icon or image in your mind. Does Pat look vaguely like a celebrity? The odds are very low that Pat will resemble a celebrity whose name is Pat. But maybe there's a passing resemblance to John Wayne. Picture John Wayne on his horse. Cowboys like to pat their horses on the mane or the rump . . . pat the horse . . . Pat.

Word association techniques can use anything that works in your mind and your imagination. If matching Pat up with a celebrity doesn't work, then use elements from your own memories of holidays, buildings, friends, food, or whatever else you have permanently locked in your mind, to which you can attach the person's name. You certainly don't have to reveal the specific association to the person; in fact, it's wise to keep that information entirely to yourself.

In addition, make sure you can see the color of Pat's eyes. This ensures you make direct eye contact, which is the heart and soul of interpersonal communication. If Pat has green eyes, then picture John Wayne in a green hat.

Many experts in interpersonal relations and sales skills have said that the sweetest music that a person can hear is their own name. If you can remember the name of a new acquaintance and use it in saying your goodbyes, you will form a lasting positive impression.

What does this have to do with time management? Word association is about avoiding delay by matching items usually stored in short-term memory to "anchors" living in long-term memory. Such speed tricks allow you to start on productive work immediately and avoid wasting precious time trying to remember. Essentially, it is the mnemonic equivalent of the 60-second workspace.

10

The Return of the Two-Pound Bucket: Constraints

B ack in Chapter 1, we looked at the merits of the two-pound bucket as a metaphor for the fixed volume of time that we are all given. The trick, it was said, was not in wishing for a bigger bucket, but in learning how to fill it correctly.

 Well, the two-pound bucket is back, with a second lesson. Suppose you are back in my yard, with some of your colleagues. I point out a barrel of water in the corner of the yard and inform you that to get paid today, you'll need to get all the water from the barrel, transport it across the yard, and pour it into another container. There are no pumps and no hoses available, and the full barrel is too heavy to lift, roll, or otherwise move. All you have is the two-pound bucket.

It would seem that the most practical way to move the water would be to stand an arm's length apart, forming a human chain from the barrel up to the container. By passing the bucket among you, the water will be transported and you will all be paid.

Now, this will be a time-consuming process, but it's the only way to get the job done. Besides, as each person is doing just a small part of the work, you will all share in a balance between work and rest. Furthermore, if the person at the end of the line pours the water into the container, then throws the empty bucket back down to the person at the barrel, you can save half of the bucket-passing time.

In this sense, a two-pound bucket is an analogy for identifying the constraints and strengths of a situation and eliciting positive change. Sure, we would like more buckets on hand. Maybe even a hose, or a forklift truck. But all you have is a single bucket. Do you perceive that bucket as a tool that will help you get the water to its goal, or do you view the entire scenario as an impossible one?

The two-pound bucket is a constraint, as is the lack of any other tools. So, too, is the number of laborers at your disposal, as well as their ability to plan, to work, and to cooperate.

Constraints are not a negative thing. Accepting the constraints of your situation does not run counter to the teachers, the mentors, and the motivational and inspirational speakers who may have told you in the past that you can achieve whatever you set your mind to. In fact, constraints support this ideal. People who talk of personal fulfillment and goal-setting generally speak of the kinds of things you can achieve if you apply your mind, your body, and your soul toward them. You have to work with what you've got, play the cards you're dealt. Constraints help to define our operating boundaries. They are credible markers of achievement and potential that come in very handy when the realities of life stand up and attempt to rob you of your optimism.

Identify, accept, and work with the constraints of your existence. If some can be changed or eliminated, then set about doing so. But true empowerment comes not from a temporary aura of blind enthusiasm, nor from a quixotic crusade. It comes from working with the tools around you and accepting the constraints of your situation. Acceptance of the constraints of a project is not a defeatist proposition. Rather, it is a positive, pragmatic tool for success.

The return of the two-pound bucket takes form as the figurehead for the notion of "constraints" — those things that hold us back, yet at the same time define clearly our operating parameters and project walls.

Time: The Ultimate Constraint

Time is fixed. There are 24 hours per day: no more, no less. It's the two-pound bucket, pure and simple. There will always be another day. Not everything can be completed in a single day; in fact it's a wasted effort to try. Planning allows you to decide what should be completed today and what can be planned for tomorrow. Choose what is important and do that first. Further, keep in mind that most things can wait. Don't fall victim to assuming that every task on your list must be completed immediately. There's only one of you, and you can do only one thing at a time. Do one thing completely before moving on.

You Are Your Own Constraint — And That's Okay

You can only do so much in one day. No matter how much you have to do, no matter how much pressure is on you to do more, no matter how willing you are to take on more or to help others, you are a fixed commodity with a finite measure of energy, ability, and time. Something's got to give. People who drive themselves to the edge have to pay themselves back, and soon. If you work 14 hours one day, don't expect to be able to give 100 percent the next day, and the day after that. You just can't do it. Working beyond your allotted capacity invites reduced quality and performance, as well as burnout, illness, and injury. Accept the fact that you are both your greatest asset and your greatest constraint. Work with that knowledge, and plan for productivity within those parameters.

The Day: Don't Miss a Pit Stop

Earlier in this book (see Chapter 7), I describe the three periods in a day: work, non-work, and sleep. Each must be used to its utmost potential. None must be used at the expense of the other. There is no extra room. If one of the three expands, the other two might give way temporarily, but your body will immediately seek to rebalance. Avoid the temptation to overwork except in rare crisis situations. Realize that balance between the three slices is not merely nice to have, it is a must-have.

Race-car drivers are under enormous pressure to win. Large groups of people have a lot riding on their victory. So, no matter how close the race is, every driver must come in on a regular basis for a pit stop. That two-minute diversion is necessary for obvious reasons: if you don't fill up now, your car will stop running soon. There is no way you can plead with a dry fuel tank to continue for a few more laps. Giving up that time to refuel the car, time that could have been spent strategically moving ahead, increasing the lead, is an accepted constraint for race-car drivers. It's a necessary component for continued success. The same must be said about you and your day: time allotted for maintenance and balance is a constraint that cannot be bartered away at the first sign of trouble. It should instead be factored in as a ground rule for personal effectiveness.

Technology

Technology is another constraint. The tools of our information age have become a staple of our existence. Once in a while, a major incident such as a computer virus or a solar flare reminds us of two things: that we are absolutely dependent on the machines we have built to serve us, and that they often don't work the way we want them to. Our machines take up our time when they need repairs or upgrades. Employees require training and practice on new technologies, and while they are learning they are working at less-than-optimum potential. Basically, it comes down to the fact that technology must be recognized as a constraint when planning your day, your week, and your life.

The Dynamics of the Work Environment

The principles of time management covered in this book *do* work. They work well. But all advice must be carefully construed to match the environment in which you work. Being strict about maintaining a Keystone Period is a good thing, and being firm about employing it is productive, but be sure at the same time to be sensitive to your office culture.

A good deal of success in business life is a result of the amount of interaction and networking that you employ to maintain visibility, approachability, and likeability. It is not merely enough to be productive. One must be seen to be productive, and one must continue to "sell" oneself even after having been hired. There is a currency of credibility that makes some people stand out beyond others. It manifests itself behind adjectives such as "charismatic" and "dynamic," and tends to point out those kinds of people who have an impact on everyone.

As you implement your time management techniques, take care to integrate your plan with sensitivity toward the status quo, and at the same time, share the principles with others. Encourage colleagues and superiors to practice Cool Time, to schedule Keystone Periods, and to focus on more proactive meetings. Remember to communicate to your colleagues and superiors that your goals are the same: efficient use of your time and talents for the benefit of the company and yourself. But also accept that they may not understand or agree with the way you choose to work. This will have an impact on the degree to which you will be able to implement time management techniques into your day, as well as the speed with which you can integrate them.

Your people, then, are project constraints. That is not a negative term, nor is it defeatist. It simply states that you can only work with what you have. Whether you work in a large company or a small firm, or even if you are self-employed, you have to work and interact with other people. Some of these people do not share your priorities, as their time management skills are not as developed. Some people will never be able to plan or manage their time properly, and even if they're capable on that front, they may be unable to match your standards. This may be due to work or family pressures, a different metabolism, or simply less natural capacity for time management and organizational techniques.

They are different people, and this must be factored into any and every project upon which you work. Take the "team project" as an example. In my discussion of project management in Chapter 4, I state that you cannot count on eight solid hours of work from a colleague simply because you think you are owed that much: the dynamics of people and work make it closer to two or three hours. A professional project manager recognizes the constraints that comprise a project and plans the project accordingly. People will always be a legitimate constraint on all of your projects, including the overall project called "day-to-day work." More can be achieved by accepting and planning for this than by trying to fight it.

Avoid ineffective delegation and no delegation. For some, viewing people as project constraints results in a temptation to bypass these people and take on their tasks, thus living up to the maxim "If you want something done right, you've got to do it yourself." As hard as it is to let go of certain parts of a project, your time and talents are probably best invested elsewhere. An efficient project manager knows enough to take the time to plan and to factor in the strengths and weaknesses of the resources available. Delegating tasks to other members of a team means freeing yourself for the tasks of a more specific nature, including managing the project. Take the Bird's-Eye View. Step back and observe how your energies and abilities can be best used in the time available. Don't jump into the trenches yourself, or you may never get out.

Choose the right person. Match tasks to team members, taking into consideration their skills, schedules, competing priorities, and vacation days. Often, in an organization where numerous projects happen concurrently, there emerges a person who is very capable of performing certain tasks or undertaking certain responsibilities. This person becomes, in the minds of all project managers, the "star player" without whom no project will be successful. The dangers of depending on a star player are numerous. The star player may suddenly become unavailable, thus impacting your project's timeline negatively, and far outweighing the positive impact the person's talents could have provided. Also, star players and their preferential treatment can impact negatively on the solidarity of a team effort. Other team members are usually available to perform at equal or similar levels of competence — it is up to you as team leader to identify or foster such a person.

Give clear instructions. Make sure the person to whom you have assigned a task clearly understands that task. Assume nothing. Ask that person to repeat it to you. This is not being patronizing; it is merely part of effective communication. Think, for example, of a surgeon calling for a tool: the surgeon states the name of the implement required. Then the O.R. assistant retrieves the tool, repeats the name of the tool, and places it into the hand of the surgeon with a particular amount of force and in a specific manner to ensure both parties share full understanding and agreement. In addition to insisting on a full understanding of the task assigned, ensure your delegate has the name of someone to contact in case of questions, so as to avoid delay and hesitation brought on by indecisiveness or fear of making a mistake.

When kicking off a major project, it is shrewd on the part of the project manager to provide every team member with a copy of the "Project Contact Book," a small booklet or file that lists the names, phone numbers, and roles of every member of the team.

Centralize your communications using the Web. Whether on the company intranet or your own private Web page, a running play-by-play of the project — including deadlines, explanations, praise for jobs well done, and a suggestion box — can be put up quite easily with nothing more than word-processing software. A centralized communications post gives people a resource and cuts down on the amount of "hand-holding" needed, thus assisting in the timely completion of the tasks that make up the project.

Give commensurate authority. Allow people the authority to go ahead with their part of the plan. If they are armed with clear instructions and a clear channel of communication, tell them to get started and allow them a certain amount of decision-making authority. In project management, the kick-off phase starts just as the project gets underway, well after the major planning has happened. This kick-off, usually in the form of a small celebration (a ribbon-cutting ceremony, for example), gives all team members a sense of momentum and authority with which to start their tasks. This should be formalized and planned for as a key success factor when dealing with multi-person projects.

Follow up. Make sure you are there to answer questions and provide leadership. You can accomplished this best through face-to-face meetings in which you can see the progress of the individual team members. It can also be achieved via e-mail or the project Web page.

Support and coach. Leadership is the art of getting people to want to do what you want them to do. If you are managing a project (including the project called "day-to-day office work"), one of the constraints to factor in is supporting and leading your team members. Of course this takes time. It's a project constraint. It's the structure that supports the body of the project. It represents wise and strategic usage of your time and the time of others.

Keep your project goals visible. Make sure you and every member of your team remembers the goal of the project so as not to get sidetracked. Sometimes, circumstances force the goals to change. It is better to make sure everyone learns about such changes quickly and officially. The definition of project management can be brought down to two words: planning and communication. Planning will define your goals; communication will ensure they stay visible.

In the day-to-day corporate context of time management, where people have their own responsibilities and no specific project seems to exist, it may help to remind everyone of the project called "your company." These goals are nestled within five-year plans, departmental strategies, and employee job descriptions. They should be reviewed regularly and actively. Progress comes from leadership. Leadership rides on shared vision.

Use all available tools. Ensure you and your people are using the tools at hand to the best of everyone's abilities. Most business applications, such as word-processing software, spreadsheets, presentation software, the Internet, and business-to-business e-commerce solutions, are vastly underused. Time spent training people in the efficient use of business tools is time wisely invested. It will return dividends in the form of efficient, productive work and well-managed time.

Set deadlines. For things to be real, they must be on paper. For projects to be real, they must have real deadlines. Thorough project planning, including planning backwards, from the deadline date to the present day, is the only way to get a Bird's-Eye View of the entire project. Make sure everybody knows the deadlines. Update your project plan once a day. Avoid drifting into obscurity and delay.

Ask for and expect reports and clear communication from your team. As you make them aware of their commensurate authority, ensure they in turn understand the necessity for reporting back their progress and problems. Remind them (if you have to) that this is not about a power trip, nor is it about being in love with piles of paper. It's about running a smooth operation, each part of which must account for itself on a daily basis.

Don't give in to your ego. Accepting people as constraints can be difficult. Motivated people often lack the patience or desire to have to deal with others. It's difficult to let go of total ownership of a project. Many of us feel we are the only ones suited to take on a particular task, and we fear that a departure from that rule will result in erosion of authority and stature. We feel anxiety about possible mistakes that might cloud our desire for perfection. You ask yourself, "Will this person do it right? Will I have to follow his or her every step and correct where he or she goes wrong? Does this person have the skills, the experience, and the ability to take on the task I'm assigning?" The only way you can answer this question is to let them go and do the task you have assigned, while you plan and allow for the constraints of the job. Time management within a team is an exercise in wise and effective delegation.

The Dynamics of the Day

This book starts by pointing out that time itself is unmanageable — it is rather the management of ourselves throughout time that generates success. Therefore, as you plan and break up the day into its respective, productive, healthy segments, consider the landscape that lies before you.

Mornings

Some people are morning people; others are not. From a purely biological point of view, humans do seem to operate better and are therefore more productive in the morning. The peak period of the morning is from 9:00 to 9:30, from which point our metabolisms spiral downward toward evening.

Should you plan the mornings for meetings or for work? Should you plan your Keystone Period for the morning and take advantage of your personal energy to maximize productivity, or plan meetings for the morning, and thereby take advantage of everyone's energy? Frankly, I think people should aim to get their own work done in this period — in fact, it should be made an office rule. Though each person's office situation may differ, it would be something along the lines of this: "everybody has a Keystone Period from 9:30 to 11:30 each day, and no one takes calls except the receptionist." Sound drastic? I think you'll find a sharp increase in productivity across the board, which in turn will help to energize the meetings scheduled for later that day.

You may disagree and think morning meetings would be better, or perhaps a combination — morning meetings some days, morning Keystone Periods other days — would best suit the people in your company. This, of course, is your decision, and only you know the dynamics of your workplace.

But your plan will be supported by the wisdom and the understanding of the dynamics of the day. We cannot change our metabolisms, but you can stand on your Emotional Bedrock (see the next chapter). Whether you are or aren't a morning person, if you can identify these traits in your colleagues, the best you can do is to factor metabolism as a constraint. Factor this knowledge into your I-Beam Review, and use it when scheduling meetings, Keystone Periods, and projects.

The Entire Day

We have seen that people work differently as the hours roll on. Understanding the dynamics of the day means understanding how other people work, not just how you work. We all have metabolic ebbs and flows: times when energy is high and times when it is much lower. It's not our fault — we're just made that way.

The chief constraint of the day, at least from a physiological perspective, is the post-lunch doldrums. These are the result of our body's cyclical mirroring of the deep-sleep period of 1:30 to 3:00 a.m. Many cultures, especially in hotter climates, have for centuries dealt with this built-in need for sleep by having a siesta of some sort. They close their stores and businesses and snooze it off. But in North America, we have opted, as a culture, to battle on through the long afternoon.

Winston Churchill insisted on a regular afternoon nap, stating that the only excuse he would allow for its interruption would be a matter of the "gravest national urgency," which he defined quite simply as nothing less than the armed invasion of the British Isles.

The afternoon trough is not a great time for work, meetings, learning, or anything. If you are ever asked to give a speech or presentation, it is best to try to make sure you're not scheduled for this period. But given that there are only about eight hours in the average workday to choose from, we don't have much choice.

Therefore, the efficient time manager views the sluggishness of the afternoon as a project constraint. Activities scheduled for that period must be supplemented by plenty of light, fresh air, and good circulation. Have plenty of water and fruit juice on hand, and schedule breaks every hour. Good work can be done during this trough period, but it is to the benefit of everyone to cater to the metabolic needs of all involved.

Working After 5:00 P.M. — and the Dreaded All-Nighter

Working after hours is half as productive as working during the day. Though there will always be instances where we have to put in some overtime, the mind and body need their rest and will attempt to get it from you regardless of your motivations. Recalling the balance chart in Chapter 7, what you borrow from the non-work and sleep slices of your day will have to be paid back. If you work until midnight, or even 8:00 p.m., you will not be at your best the next day. If you're asked to work a late night, then there's not a lot of point in showing up at the office at 8:00 a.m. the next day, since your body and mind will be collecting on the loan, leaving you working at reduced capacity.

Studies have shown that the human body never adjusts to night shifts. We are creatures of the day, governed by our circadian rhythm, and have been for millions of years. People often feel cold when working the graveyard shift. This is natural. During the night hours, the body's core temperature is lower — it's expecting sleep. It goes ahead with at least part of its nightly shutdown, even if you are still at your desk. *Microsleep* is a term used to describe momentary periods of shutdown experienced by all humans during waking hours. Tests performed on airline pilots and others have shown that microsleep happens for a few seconds every 90 minutes. This has only been discovered recently, through the use of electroencephalographs (EEGs) and other technologies. Those who work during the night experience higher incidences of microsleep, which in turn interferes with thought processes and personal energy, and further slows the pace of work.

If you must burn the midnight oil, try to plan to have the next day — or at least the next morning — off to recuperate. Your mind and body will be taking it off whether you like it or not.

Proactive project planning and a regular review of your work-load through the I-Beam Review and Bird's-Eye View are the best methods for avoiding all-nighters. If the work you have to do was not foreseen, you will be doing yourself a greater favor in rescheduling it, getting the rest and relaxation you deserve, and then attacking it fresh and rested tomorrow. If that's not possible and there is no choice but to pull an all-nighter, try to work along with, rather than against, your body's demands. Make sure to have enough food, and healthy food at that. The high carbohydrate levels found in pizza and other fast foods will just make you tired faster. Coffee or tea will provide a welcome boost, but make sure you also have access to plenty of fresh water.

Keep a sweatshirt or light sweater handy, as you will start to feel colder as the night sets in and your body starts its descent into its circadian depths. Make sure to stand up and stretch once an hour. Set a timer to remind you. Sixty seconds of deep breathing and knee bends will keep blood and oxygen flowing. Finally, if you work in an office building, make sure to put your pass card or key in your pocket. Nothing is worse than heading out to the washroom or to get a coffee at 1:00 a.m. during a high-pressure all-nighter only to find yourself locked out.

The Week and the Month

Which days are more productive? As professionals, we work hard and conscientiously and put in a great many hours at the office. But thanks to constant distractions, meetings, and overlapping tasks, our work hours are often uneven in their levels of productivity. Not only is this true throughout the day, but there are also rhythms to our weeks, months, and year, all of which impact the amount of work we can expect from ourselves and our colleagues.

From a time management perspective, this reality means our

planning must take into account the constraints of the Western working year.

Mondays, for example, are a time to get back into gear after the weekend. In many cases, people arrive back to work some-what refreshed and ready to start again, but a good deal of their renewed mental and physical energy is spent during the first half of the day just getting back up to speed. This rebuilding of momentum means working at a reduced potential as people face an onslaught of work after a period of rest. I call this the "week-end effect."

Also, don't expect a full day from people on a Friday. Most people are starting to focus on the weekend, and by 2:00 p.m. many are already mentally "out the door and on their way." Okay, maybe this is not you, but this does describe many of your colleagues and clients, and that's important to consider when planning meetings or setting deadlines. Some managers like to schedule meetings for 4:00 on a Friday afternoon to ensure a punctual end. That's a little harsh, in my opinion, but it serves to underline the fact that no one likes to stay late on a Friday, nor should they have to. This anticipatory wind-down, and its result-ant reduction in productivity, is also part of the "weekend effect."

Public Holidays: The Seven-Day Weekend
A long weekend is a well-deserved rest that contributes greatly to our need for balance. But the problem with long weekends from a time management perspective is that people start their count-downs on the Monday prior. It's a little easier to get out of bed that morning knowing a long weekend is coming up. This means that people will experience a slow, week-long decline in produc-tivity, mentally "checking out" by noon on Thursday as the long weekend enters and overtakes their thoughts.

Even the most earnest and dedicated professional will think twice before starting on a new project at 3:00 p.m. on the Friday before a long weekend, especially if it means trying to contact someone by phone. Sales calls are not so productive on a Friday as they are on other days. It's just not the time to be starting things. Unfortunately, Friday comprises 20 percent of the available time in an average workweek. When people have their minds on the long weekend, they are working at less than 100 percent between noon on Thursday and noon on Monday, which adds up to another full day of work.

There are ten official holiday days in a North American business year. When you add these ten days to the ten business days of "sub-par" consciousness, that equals four full business weeks when people are not available to do work.

Christmas and the Holiday Season

The annual Christmas holiday season takes the notion of "lost work" and stretches it for weeks. People's minds generally start to gravitate away from work and toward holiday festivities by December 15th, and do not fully recover until the first week of January. They are distracted by plans for office and home parties. Lunch hours are stretched to allow for shopping and standing in lines, and businesses other than retail generally experience a plague of mental and physical absenteeism.

These festivities are well deserved, of course, and holidays have been held around this time of year for thousands of years. However, the effective time manager, when planning a multi-month project or assessing the day-to-day tasks of the office, must take into account the severe drop in productivity and potential that coincides with the holiday season.

The February Blahs

The post-holiday season ushers in the February blahs. A combination of the negative physical reaction brought on by the cold and the diminished daylight, as well as the emotional reaction to the post-holiday anticlimax, means that many people are not going to be working to their full potential at these times either. Sometimes this escalates into chronic seasonal affective disorder (SAD).

Summer Holidays

During the summer months, people take their holidays, or at least have their minds on their holidays. Again, the momentum of business seems to slow down. Trying to plan meetings and projects around the holiday schedules of an office full of people can be a daunting task and a real project constraint.

Halloween

Though it's not registered as a statutory holiday, October 31st is unique in the Western business calendar in that it is a day when a disproportionate number of people do actually go home on time to accommodate a higher priority: spending Halloween night with the kids. Even for those without young children, the effects are noticeable: traffic chaos, disappearing colleagues, and reduced productivity. My suggestion: leave work at 3:00 p.m. on October 31st.

On the next page is a semi-scientific chart intended to demonstrate how the dynamics of the workday impact our work year. It sometimes helps to bring greater gravity to the idea of effective project planning and time management. (Numbers and estimations are generalized, and rounded off for convenience.)

There are 365 days in a year.	**365**
104 days are weekends.	**-104**
Assume 18 days for personal holidays and sick days.	**-18**
Mondays and Fridays lose 20 percent of their productivity potential due to the "weekend effect." Not counting personal and public holidays, assume 45 Mondays and 45 Fridays per year. Twenty percent of 90 days = 18 days.	**-18**
Work days available	**215**
Time given over to actual work (see "The Work Habits of the Average Human," Chapter 6): 25 percent of 215 days	**53.75**
Productivity in terms of metabolic decline over the course of the day (averages a 75 percent working capacity): 75 percent of 53.75 days	**40.3**

There you have it: just over 40 days of work a year.

Remember, this chart is not scientific. It serves, however, to make a point about how much work we do, and how much work we think we do. Sometime in early February next year, pat yourself on the back for having already completed your "work year"!

11

Emotional Bedrock: Acceptance and Implementation

I have pointed out at many junctures in this book that the principles of effective time management are neither difficult nor revolutionary. They consist of straightforward techniques in planning, communication, and accepting and working with constraints. The figurehead for this section, then, is bedrock — or more precisely, Emotional Bedrock. In the real world, bedrock is the solid, underlying level of rock upon which buildings can be erected. For our purposes in time management, it refers to an inner conviction that what you are doing is right — not because one single book or seminar told you so, but because the techniques upon which this book is based are time-honored and proven. They stretch back over the decades of the 20th century, with their roots firmly planted in project management.

When it comes time to explain to your manager why you want to close your door for two hours a day, or why you feel entitled to go home at 6:00 p.m. instead of starting on another project, or why your estimation of a project's timeline factors in only two hours per day of productivity rather than nine, or why you insist that a meeting starts and ends at its posted time, I want you to be able to stand on the bedrock of under-

> **Of All the Gin Joints in the World . . .**
>
> Julius Epstein, along with his twin brother, Philip, wrote some of the most famous screenplays in Hollywood history, including *Casablanca*.
>
> A temporary illness in the 1940s forced the studio to give Mr. Epstein permission to work from home on the screenplay, which he did. As a result, he was able to complete the work in half the time.
>
> He worked full-out for two hours a day. Any more than that, he said, just brought inferior quality. The rest of the time, he played tennis or golf.
>
> Okay, so we don't all have tennis courts in our backyards, but doesn't it help to prove a point? Two hours of focus is better than ten hours of blur.

standing that these principles are right, and do work. As you seek to explain why these time management principles should be employed, you can remind your manager that you're both on the same side. Your mutual desired goal is improved productivity without added cost. You can also remind your manager (and yourself) that you are not alone. There are hundreds of thousands of professionals out there for whom a calculated, regimented time management schedule has enhanced both professional productivity and home life.

Caution: Now, I must caution you that these explanations can only go so far. Only you know the conditions and relationships in your workplace. Some of your time management principles may be accepted and integrated. In some situations, however, it would be dangerous to continue the contest. In this case, you must accept your employer and its management strategy as a constraint and work around it.

Is Cool Time Just a Trend? A Fad?

As you consider whether to accept principles such as the Keystone Period into your own life, you may be wondering why these techniques aren't already being employed in the workplace, and whether attempting to implement them would be dangerous.

I would suggest to you that there are two consistencies to consider here. One is that the diligent application of a technique, such as any of those offered in this book — or that of a fitness, nutrition, or investment program — does indeed work, but it takes time and requires that you stick with the plan, review it regularly, and expend some effort in keeping on course.

The other consistency is that of human nature to drift back toward a comfort zone of reduced effort and complexity. Programs launched with great fanfare and promise tend to dissolve if they are not properly maintained. When faced with continued crises, pressures, and distractions, people find they just do not have the time to give to such maintenance. So the program disappears, leaving only a memory of how difficult it was, a memory that will serve to thwart further attempts in this area.

Time management can change your life in small or large ways. It requires acceptance from you and the people around you to make it work.

Objections to Time Management

Nobody appreciates being told how to act. Books on time management or on any other organizational technique often force people to reassess habits and priorities. To some, this seems to take all the fun out of life. Since effective time management requires a certain amount of change and cultivation, it is up to you to confront your own objections and weigh the potential benefits against the priorities and practicalities of life.

It is also necessary to keep the suggestions in this book balanced against the realities of your workplace and family life. Though the techniques mentioned would serve an entire office well, changes should be introduced at a calculated pace. It is important to avoid creating a scenario that is potentially harmful to your health, safety, and career, as well as to those of your colleagues. Here are some of the more common reactions to time management principles. How many can you relate to?

- Time management doesn't allow for spontaneity — I'm the spontaneous type.
- It's only good for people in a routine — that's not me.
- It may work for others, but it simply won't work here — our environment is too different.
- I have no time to put together a plan.
- I work better under pressure — I'm a last-minute kind of person.
- When I need to, I just work harder — hard work equals more work.
- I'm already organized and I'm doing just fine / I have a system — I've used it for years.

These objections are all perfectly sound. People are conservative by nature. Change generates fear of the unknown, a fear of failure or of being seen to fail. This fear goes back all the way to the early days of our evolutionary history. Like the rest of our metabolisms, it cannot be changed so much as understood and properly channeled. Now have a look at this list again, but this time with some possible responses:

Time management doesn't allow for spontaneity — I'm the spontaneous type. Time management does allow for spontaneity. In fact, it's perfect for spontaneity, since it allows "free time" to exist. By keeping the day in order and a day plan in mind, spontaneous activities can occur without endangering or forgetting the fixed activities and priorities of the day. Being able to take some time for yourself is essential, but in the real world this can only truly work if the tasks of the day are complete, or at least planned clearly.

It's only good for people in a routine — that's not me. Everyone has a routine. Some routines are just more obvious than others. A person who does shift work, or someone who has a fixed list of tasks to accomplish day in and day out, has his or her routine clearly mapped out. However, we all have a routine — by the very nature of the 24-hour clock and our metabolic and social cycles of days, weeks, and months. The first stage in effective time management is to step back, observe the constants and standards in your life, and then recognize the routine in which you operate. Then, like a fish suddenly discovering the water in which it lives, the patterns of your existence will emerge for you to manipulate and finesse. If you can't identify any distinct routine happening on a daily basis, step back and observe your activities over a week or a month. Your routine will emerge, and will serve as the foundation for your time management plans.

It may work for others, but it simply won't work here — our environment is too different. Every environment is different. Every environment has its routine. Every office thinks theirs is the only one with unique pressures and requirements that make any time management regimen unworkable. Periods of apparent chaos may come and go regularly, and there will be crises and quiet times. But if you step back and observe how the work pattern of your office ebbs and flows, you will be able to refine the manner in which you spend the hours of the day.

I have no time to put together a plan. In Chapter 13, I point out that to succeed with an effective time management plan, you must both create the plan and then commit to a kickoff period. There may also be a need for a phase-in period and a review period to pick up or refine your change in work habits. The development and maintenance of a time management plan needs an initial period of commitment followed by further commitments of time simply to maintain the plan. Your planning time may entail a few minutes at the beginning and end of each day (an I-Beam Review), and an hour or so every other Sunday, observing your schedule and deciding on the time management tactics that will work for you (a Bird's-Eye View). Are you willing to do that? It may mean committing to a clean-up of your work area. Are you willing to do *that*? Without adequate planning and kickoff, your time management techniques will remain ineffective, and your goals will remain out of reach. Create the time to put together a plan.

I work better under pressure — I'm a last-minute kind of person. Nobody really works better under pressure. Pressure immobilizes higher brain functions such as rational thought, decision-making, and prioritization. It is a condition born out of stress, and it triggers a modern-day manifestation of the instinctive fight-or-flight reflex. In short, pressure instills mental panic. What makes people feel better about working under pressure is their acceptance that there is no more time left and that the deadline has struck.

By pressing our creative selves against a wall, we absolve

ourselves of the guilt that less-than-optimum performance affords, allowing the constraints of time to shoulder the blame.

Many of us were taught this during the high school, college, and/or university years, when final exams and term papers brought last-minute cramming and all-nighters, and the "pencils-down" command spurred a flurry of frantic erasing, guessing, and filling-in. Indeed, much of academic life seems to emphasize and encourage cramming, procrastination, and requests for deadline extensions.

Pressure erodes quality. A well-planned project of any sort always leaves room for reflection, strategy, and improvement. If you have the luxury of starting a project or task from square one, ensure that the last third of the project timeline is for revision, corrections, and add-ons. Plan adequately for the unexpected. By planning for revisions and corrections, you can avoid "last-minute syndrome" and truly enjoy the benefits of heightened productivity, reduced stress, and increased control over your work and leisure time.

When I need to, I just work harder — hard work equals more work. Working without planning is like working with an improperly harnessed ox or an unsharpened blade. Huge amounts of misplaced energy will not yield quality work — and sometimes will not yield any product at all. While it may serve to absolve the conscience temporarily, the act of putting in longer hours or requesting more productivity from yourself or your staff in a time-critical situation merely guarantees sub-par performance. By pushing the boundaries of the work-life balance chart (see Chapter 7), you yield less productivity than you would in a properly planned and paced day. You cannot make bread rise twice as fast by putting in twice as much yeast.

I'm already organized, and I'm doing just fine / I have a system — I've used it for years. If you have a system and that system works for you and your colleagues in a satisfactory way, then congratulations are in order. Still, take a moment to observe your current work environment and note whether certain areas are in need of improvement. Nobody likes to be told what to do, and change can feel threatening. It is likely, however, that your current system has room for improvement. To be able to embrace change, it is necessary to confront your objections. Note any feelings or resistance you may feel toward time management and assess whether your arguments can be countered, or whether your current way of doing things is adequate.

Time Management and Senior Management

All the time management and organizational skills in the world may appear insignificant and forgettable if your manager fails to see their potential. The suggestions in this chapter, as with those in all the other chapters, are simply guidelines. Only you know your situation, and your relationship with your manager and your company. Your manager has a manager — everyone has someone higher up the ladder to whom they must report. Diplomacy, tact, and foresight must be employed when integrating effective time management into the existing work sphere.

Most companies and their managers are looking for maximum productivity, minimum costs, and general advancement of their segment of the company, at least in the eyes of their superiors. Change, especially when initiated from the field rather than from the directors, can be viewed suspiciously or welcomed warmly, depending on the outlook of the company's management. In the interest of walking a mile in your manager's shoes, he or she may already be working to a project plan, and the insertion of a radical new time management process may pose a threat to that plan's current structure.

Remind your manager that the time management techniques described in this book have been devised with the goal of personal and professional improvement. When applied correctly, they will enhance your productivity in practical, measurable ways. The points below are included to help you phrase constructive arguments in the face of opposition to your new time management techniques. They will also prove useful if you find yourself continually overloaded with work, to the point where it will be impossible to complete — regardless of what time management tools are used.

Remember that you have been hired as a professional. You have a job to do, and you are expected to do it correctly and professionally. By embracing time management techniques, you are improving the way in which you work. Explain the reasoning behind planned time management to your manager. Focus on the results and deliver a vision of maximized productivity. Make your manager aware of the exact principles you intend to use, such as a Keystone Period, or the importance of being able to go home at a decent hour, and remind him or her that these techniques are in place in the interest of self-improvement and heightened productivity to the company.

There is only so much a person can do in one day. No one person can do an impossible amount of work. Often, however, conflicting tasks and crises become the norm. This is unhealthy, impractical, and counterproductive. If too much comes across your desk, no matter how dedicated you may be, there is still a fixed amount you can achieve. Moving beyond that boundary invites errors, delays, and illness.

Ask your manager to help you prioritize your tasks. If ten items on your clearly written To-Do list are all marked top priority, it is a good idea for you and your manager to determine together which of these top priorities is to be the actual "number-one" priority, and which can be put by the wayside. Allow your manager to help in the prioritization process and to take some of the responsibility. It's part of a manager's role to manage. Use the priority grid and SMARTS test in Chapter 4 to make sound prioritization decisions.

Keep your Active Agenda in clear view. Not only does this help you to remain focused on your time management techniques, it is also a strong ally when discussing workloads. Your manager may not be able to see the world through your eyes. As a manager of other people it is easy to lose track of all the tasks that have been assigned. By having a clearly laid-out daily plan in written form, you will be better able to remind your manager of the tasks currently on your plate.

Use your written day plans for credibility. A clear history of your workload for today, tomorrow, the past, and the future testifies to your productivity, abilities, and work ethic. A good manager would be foolish to risk losing an organized employee. This is strong currency in the negotiation of workloads and deadlines.

Insist on training as a top priority. A great deal of time is wasted due to a lack of experience with the tools of the trade. Word-processing software, spreadsheet software, and the Internet can swallow huge amounts of time simply because staff members are not sufficiently familiar with their workings. Many organizations will spend large amounts of money buying software, computers, and other technologies, yet training is relegated to the back burner and is often first to be cut in times of fiscal retreat. However, using technology is a professional skill. Without training, it is merely a car without wheels. Being trained on a topic or technology may certainly take a few hours out of a particular workday, but the dividend comes from its efficient use for the months and years to follow.

Do not make a habit of staying late. The occasional crunch period happens to everyone once in a while, and it certainly makes sense to pull together in those situations to resolve a short-term crisis. But constant acceptance of overwork and overly long hours sends a signal to your company and to your manager that back-breaking conditions are acceptable and are the norm. Such behavior will establish a precedent from which it is hard to escape.

What makes people stay late? Why do they donate their non-work time to their company? Reasons that come back again and again include the following:

- the fear of losing one's job or seniority
- a desire to move upwards through the ranks
- personal motivation to "just get things done"
- a desire to appear as part of the team
- the fear that leaving on time will be frowned upon, even if you arrive before everyone else each morning

These pressures may be imposed from within or from your corporate culture. Either way, they represent a yoke that some managers may count on to deal with overly heavy workloads. They establish a benchmark of productivity beyond the call of duty and make that the expected level for every day.

Do not make a habit of taking work home with you. Taking work home is another dangerous precedent. Working through the evenings or on weekends is a sacrifice of your essential non-work time. More than that, it's a "donation" of that time. Keeping yourself connected to your cell phone, pager, or corporate e-mail is part of this.

If you are officially "on call" during your non-work time, then of course, remaining accessible is crucial. It's part of your job, and presumably you are compensated accordingly. Similarly, a crunch or catch-up period during which your company can count on you for your extended efforts may happen on occasion, but this should always be infrequent and exemplary.

Making yourself always "available," week in and week out, is dangerous and destructive. Resist the temptation to fall into the superhero syndrome. Being available and always ready to jump into the fray may make you feel great, important, and indispensable, but in the end it's just empty calories of esteem — the career equivalent of a chocolate donut. The quick high is soon replaced by substandard mental and physical performance due to a lack of true quality non-work time.

Do not take on more than you can do. Most of us wish we could do more in a day, but our minds and bodies are only capable of a finite amount. To push them further invites breakdown, sub-par performance, and illness. Be aware of this constraint and use it proactively. Think of the tachometer on the dashboard of your car. It shows you the maximum rpm that your engine can safely attain. There is always a red zone at the far end into which the needle should never venture, and most responsible car owners know that engine damage, not elation, is what awaits your car's engine there. Now think of yourself the same way. We all come with tachometers, but unfortunately, they're not within our line of sight. They're hidden and can be easily ignored or overruled by a misguided ego. If you red-line yourself, you will sideline yourself. It's as simple as that.

Make sure what you're doing is worth it. The money, the hours, the work. Do these things let you enjoy your family, your hobbies, your non-work time now, or is everything you're doing simply in the name of future pleasures? Stephen Covey, who is a master at helping people visualize priorities in the midst of their busy lives, relates a story about two neighbors in *The Seven Habits of Highly Effective People*. One of them expended much time and money in keeping his lawn pristine, green, and weed-free, to the point that no one was allowed to walk on it. The other neighbor, however, let his children and their friends play on the lawn to the point at which it became worn, patchy, and certainly less than perfect-looking. The first neighbor asked him, "How can you stand allowing your lawn to be damaged and used like that?" The second neighbor replied simply, "In ten years, the grass will still be here, but these children won't."

This chapter on Emotional Bedrock is not about encouraging professionals to work to rule. It is instead about "working to reason." No matter how motivated you may be, your physical and mental selves need maintenance, and you have the professional responsibility, obligation, and right to ensure that this happens.

12

Tools of the Trade

In the section "Technology Is a Tool, Not a Solution" in Chapter 6, I discuss how the technologies available to us do not always work in the ways they are supposed to. Malfunctions, confusion, and failures lead to delay, frustration, and stress. They seem to happen at precisely the wrong time: printers jam while you're hurrying to print a report, computers freeze on the last paragraph of a document that has yet to be saved, networks go down on the day you desperately need access.

When these tools fail us, stress is the result. Since we depend so heavily on them, a simple malfunction can ruin everything. But everyone who's ever hit his or her thumb with a hammer knows that the hammer itself is not entirely to blame. Though office technology often is the culprit and is prone to failure in numerous ways, this should not come as a complete surprise. In fact, office technologies are constraints. They are elements in your life that function in a fashion slightly different from what you might like.

There are two kinds of action you can employ to ensure technology works with you, not against you — especially when things get busy: "preemptive time management with tools" and "active time management with tools."

Preemptive Time Management with Tools

Save your work regularly. Computers crash, software freezes. It's an issue that just won't go away. Whatever you're working on, save your work every ten minutes or after every milestone (e.g., after each column of numbers entered on a spreadsheet, or after each paragraph typed into a report). It's not neurotic to save so often. It is so much easier to handle a computer freeze knowing that only a negligible amount of work will be lost.

Make backups of everything. Keep duplicate files of your most important work on a separate disk, and also on paper. If company security is an issue, keep these backups under lock and key and destroy them once the project is done. But make sure to have a hard copy of everything that is important to you. Also, make alternate backups. If your company requires you to save your data to a network drive, make a habit of saving a backup copy of your current work so it will still be accessible if the network goes down.

Factor computer problems into your project time estimates. When planning or estimating the time required to complete a task on a computer, factor in additional time for proofreading, making corrections, and restarting or logging on. Don't forget that you will also need time to print and time to deal with printing and network problems.

Learn the software. Take the time to learn the key components of whatever software you are using. You don't need to become a master of the entire application, but many problems are caused simply through inexperience. No software is as easy to use as its manufacturers claim. A couple of hours invested with a private coach in a training session, or even with an instructional book, will give you the tools to do the job quickly and efficiently.

Active Time Management with Tools

When faced with a computer, printer, or modem that stops working, most people immediately leap to "fixing" the problem. This is an example of urgency taking over in place of importance. It is better to remember that the technology is being used as a tool for the creation of a product or service that represents your expertise. The technology itself is therefore of secondary priority. Consider some of the following alternatives:

Take a deep breath and step out of "panic mode." Nothing positive gets done when you're panicking. If you hear yourself saying, "I can't get anything else done until this copier is fixed," stop for a moment and take a Bird's-Eye View. Recognize that your project will get done; you will succeed, even in the face of technology failure. Simple roadblocks will not be enough to stop you. Count to ten, then look around and assess what can be done next. Don't let the shock of interrupted momentum inject you with panic or anger, and don't let these feelings become contagious. Unless you are performing life-saving surgery, you have a few moments to step back and collect your thoughts.

Focus on the product, not the tool. If the technology failure isn't something you can fix right away, turn to an alternate source of technology to get the job done. If your fax software doesn't work because of a faulty modem, turn to a regular fax machine instead. If your computer projector has stopped working moments before a big presentation, use a whiteboard instead. If a disk is unreadable, return to a previous backup on a different disk, or retrieve files stored away in a paper folder. Backups and contingency planning are important.

Assess whether it is worth your time to fix the technology. Most of us have only a little knowledge of the workings of a computer, printer, or copier. If you can't fix the problem within ten minutes, your time is most likely better spent calling in a professional while you turn to an alternate resource.

Turn to another machine to finish your task. If another computer or copier is available, turn to it now. Focus on the urgent and top priority — getting your work done. Someone else can do the repairs.

Return to your task later, after a technician has fixed the problem. If there are no other machines available, try fixing your Active Agenda rather than fixing the machine. The task that is being held up by the machine's failure — where does it fit into your overall day plan? Return to your Active Agenda and assess what could be moved around to accommodate this change in schedule. Remember to use all of your time wisely. Assign yourself another task while the problem is being solved, and return to the first task later in the day.

Remember: You cannot shout at a machine. Well, you can, actually, but it will do little good. Frustrated people will often click the mouse repeatedly, or press a button numerous times when the machine in front of them refuses to work.

Sometimes this has no effect at all, but often, especially in the case of the mouse, it simply compounds the problem. Computers react to commands, not orders or pleading. Repeated clicks of the mouse send additional requests to an already overburdened processor. This results in further delay and frustration, since the computer will have to be rebooted to clear the jam. Your best recourse is to count to ten, step back from the problem, and work slowly at unraveling it.

Time Management in the Home Office

If you have the opportunity to work from home, either full-time or occasionally, you will enjoy unique challenges and opportunities. It's certainly pleasurable being able to commute from the kitchen to the office without taking off your slippers, but it comes at the cost of reduced social contact, a blurring of the lines between work and home life, and the threat of a complete lack of physical and mental separation. Time management in a home office has its own requirements.

Create a Designated Workspace

A designated area for work, preferably a separate room with its own telephone line, helps build a useful boundary between your work life and family life. It creates legitimacy, which is needed for effective, productive work. Though family members may be allowed in this room, it should be understood that the room is a special part of the home. While you are at work, you should be considered "at work." The pleasure of spending more of your work time in the company of your children, partner, or pets is one of the privileges of working at home. Spontaneous play periods with the children, or a non-work-related conversation with your partner, may be worth more to you than the time it takes away from productive work. But remain aware that distractions at home can be equally damaging to your productivity as distractions at the office.

Your designated workspace allows for focus. One cannot truly run a business from a dining-room table, nor should phone calls be returned with the sound of a TV blaring in the background. By designating a workspace, you are building a time-effective foundation for the work periods of your day while simultaneously enjoying the comforts of your own home.

Establish Designated Work Hours

Know when to start and when to quit. The single biggest problem with running a home-based business is that work is always nearby, and the temptation to spend just a little more time on it is strong. The hours you work are completely up to you.

One of the advantages of home-based work is the significant amount of time gained each day in not having to commute. This allows you to start work at 7:00 a.m. if you like, or sleep in if you prefer. People who work from home have a distinct two- or three-hour advantage over their commuting colleagues, and are therefore capable of achieving much more by noon than could be done in an office. In addition, the relative lack of distractions and drop-in visitors means you stand to gain a lot of additional work time throughout the day.

It is important, though, that you do stop eventually and give yourself the non-work time you deserve. Establish a rule that the office closes at 6:00 p.m. and re-opens at 8:00 a.m. Resist the temptation to return to your office room after supper to check for faxes, e-mail, or voice mail. Simply refer back to the discussion on the importance of balance in Chapter 7, and let your non-work time rebuild your strength and acuity for the next business day.

Maximize the Power of the Keystone Period

Being at home allows for fewer distractions than being at the office. This allows Keystone Periods to extend to two, three, or four hours straight! You can get a powerful amount of work done in four undisturbed hours, and the feeling of accomplishment that this brings is one of the great rewards of home-based work. Make sure to stand up and stretch at least once an hour just to keep the circulation going.

Create Your Own Work Hours

One of the best things about working from home is the freedom to choose your own hours. For example, if you have school-age children, the period between 3:30 p.m. and 4:30 p.m. may be better spent with them as they arrive home from school. Similarly, you may enjoy working out at a health club in the early afternoon, after the peak crowds have left. Whether you return to work immediately after this period or spend two hours at work from 10:00 p.m. to midnight, the scheduling of your periods of work is up to you. Providing you plan time for non-work as well as work, you will enjoy productivity and balance in healthy proportions.

Meet Regularly with Staff, Clients, or Associations, But in Cool Time

Face-to-face contact is still the most successful way of communicating. As a home-based professional, take advantage of your altered time abilities to remain time-efficient, even when travel is involved. The best way to do this is to actively plan meetings outside of rush hour. Schedule your Keystone Period for the commuting hours of the morning while everyone else is stuck on a train, bus, or highway. Then, leave the house at 10:00 a.m. to arrive in Cool Time for an 11:00 a.m. meeting. The time saved in traveling in off-peak hours is an additional benefit of home-based work.

Take Lunch

Avoid the temptation to eat at your desk. Take a break, sit outside, take the dog for a walk, and get some air. There is nothing wrong with having a lunch break while working from home — in fact there is everything right about it. Your total control over what you wish to eat is an additional Cool Time benefit, as your choices are usually healthier and less expensive than downtown food.

Get Your Own Computer, Phone Line, and Data Line

If you have family members who also require computer access time, then get your own computer for home-office use. The same goes for dedicated phone lines: Get one for voice and another for data. It is time-consuming to have to share these resources with family members. High-speed Internet access is recommended.

Accept Constraints and Plan Around Them

Working in a home office has its share of constraints, most of which concern the fact that you are on your own. For a start, you are on your own when technical problems arise. It is essential, therefore, that you have access to qualified help:

- When purchasing a new computer for your home office, choose a brand and/or retailer that offers at-home technical support or overnight delivery of replacement parts.
- Locate a qualified computer technician or coach in your area who is willing to come by on short notice.

- Keep your old machinery (computer, fax machine) handy, just in case you have to dust it off to continue working while your main system is being serviced.
- Make "backup-keeping" a key component of every business day. Making sure you have access to your data in more than one form is an act of proactive time management as it ensures that time and money are not wasted in reproducing lost data.

Using the Internet

The Internet is a great resource and a fantastic communications tool, but it can also swallow a lot of your time without you being aware of it. Time seems to move even faster when you are staring at a computer screen.

The secret to time-efficient Internet use is to invest some of your energies into mastering the technology.

People, TV, and the Internet

Try this experiment: look carefully at the face of somebody, perhaps a family member or friend, who is watching television. The face and eyes are generally passive as the information being pushed toward him or her is received.

Next, observe someone who is surfing the Internet. The person's gaze appears focused at a point deep within the monitor. Often, people are staring "into" the computer screen, making Internet usage an "active" task.

This is one reason why time seems to slip away so quickly on the Internet: there are no scheduled intervals, commercial breaks, or program changes, and for the most part we become engrossed in the information it presents to the exclusion of everything else.

Choose Two or Three Search Tools and Learn Them Thoroughly

Most people only scratch the surface when it comes to using search engines. It is discouraging when a search engine returns hundreds or thousands of pages of information, which might or might not contain the desired data. Yet this is much like a person who dislikes supermarkets or bookstores because the shelves are stocked with thousands of items that seem irrelevant and unnecessary at any given time. The trick to successful Internet research is in knowing how to navigate the space.

Choose two or three search engines that have a look and functionality that appeal to you. Try them out and see what kind of information they provide, as well as how easy it is for you to find what you're looking for. Ask colleagues and friends about the search engines they use and how satisfied they are. Read the "fine print," usually in the "Help" section of a search engine site, and learn how the search engine collects and presents information. Do they patrol the Internet and read the "metatags" (hidden keyword text on a Web site), or does the site's own staff accept submissions and manually categorize the listings? Does the search engine read the text of a Web site homepage, or does it read every word of every page? Does your search engine locate data from its own database, or does it search the databases of other search engines? All of these principles will affect the accuracy and intricacy of your search.

Learn the Syntax of the Advanced Search

Once you have chosen your search engines, you can make the most of your Internet search time by mastering the syntax of the search. Each search engine uses a computer database, which requires certain commands to operate. The most basic commands include typing in a keyword and then clicking on the "Search" button. But if you dig a little deeper, you will learn the words that make the search far more effective.

Every search engine has a page dedicated to showing you how to perform an advanced search. The link to this advanced search page is usually found near the main search panel — that horizontal rectangular window into which keywords are typed during a basic search. The link to the advanced search instructions may be labeled "Help," "Advanced Search," "Power Search," or "Tips and Tricks." Go to this page, print it, read it, learn it, and use it. The ten minutes you spend reading and learning the tricks of the advanced search will save hours of fruitless searching.

Unfortunately, each search engine has a different syntax, so you will have to do this for each of your chosen search engines.

Set a Time Limit on Your Searches

If you master the art of the advanced search at the outset, then your searches will automatically require less time. However, since the Internet can be so engrossing, it really helps to use a timer such as your watch, your PDA, or if you're working from home, the timer on your microwave oven. Set yourself a fixed period; depending on the complexity and importance of your search, this could be anywhere from five minutes to two hours. Not only will the timer help to bring you back into the real world at the end of this period, but you will also experience a greater ability to focus knowing that there is an end time to your concentrated efforts. Essentially, you make a "deal" with your body and mind: "Let me work flat out for exactly two hours," you say to yourself, "and then we'll have a rest." A fixed time limit also helps squeeze out the temptation for distraction, explained below.

Avoid Distraction

Since there is so much of everything out there on the Internet, distraction can come in many forms. A key principle of effective time management is to not fall into the distraction trap. Major sources of distraction on the Internet include these:

- **Web sites that are interesting, but not relevant to your search.** If they are personally interesting, use the Bookmark or Favorites feature of your Web browser to "snag" them, and return to these sites during a break or during your non-work period. Use the promise of revisiting these interesting sites as a reward for your current diligence and as a weapon against procrastination.

- **Web sites that seem relevant, but are not obvious.** Some Web sites may contain the text or subject for which you are searching, but it is not obvious at first glance where this information may be. Waste no time. Perform a second, internal search, using the Web site's own search engine (if it has one), and also use the "Find text on this page" feature of your own browser to root out the keywords. The point here is to avoid being distracted by "skating" back and forth across the site, hoping to come across the information by chance.

- **Web sites that are slow to load.** Even if you have high-speed access to the Internet, certain Web sites are going to load slowly due to pressures at the server end or on the Internet itself. If a page does not load in 15 seconds, stop and use the Refresh or Reload feature of your browser to request another copy. If the page still does not reload, move on to a different Web site, making a note to return to this slow site at a later time, when the log-jam has cleared.

Bookmark Useful Sites

When you locate Web sites or particular pages on a Web site that are truly relevant to your research, make sure to bookmark them using the Bookmark or Favorites command in your browser. Maximizing the use of your browser's bookmark features will save you from having to search for these pages again.

Exploit Hyperlinks

Documents created in word-processing applications automatically format e-mail addresses and Web site URLs to become hyperlinks when clicked. This means that a person reading your document on-screen, using a computer connected to the Internet, will be taken to the Web site with one single click. This has excellent results for saving time and maintaining the accuracy of corporate documents, from research manuals to annual reports to daily correspondence. Use the hyperlink feature to help save time moving in and out of the Internet.

Learn How to Zip and Unzip Files

Attachments that are overly large in size will take many minutes to upload to your mail server and then download at the other end. This is time-consuming for both parties. Using compression software can shrink files down to as little as 10 percent of their original size (depending on content). In addition, compression programs allow numerous files to be sent together, in one compact package. This saves time not only in transmission, but also in receipt — all the required files arrive together, removing the need for the recipient to search around for stragglers or request a resend.

Understand Macro Virus Warnings

If you receive a document that was created with the help of *macros* (automated tasks within a document to help speed its creation), your computer's e-mail software will alert you to that fact and warn you that macro viruses may be present. It doesn't mean that viruses have been detected. Rather, this alerts you simply to the fact that macros were used in the creation of the document, so the conditions are right for macro viruses.

Such a warning can be distressing and confusing to the average user, who then hesitates. Should I open the document? Should I return it to the sender? Should I request a second copy? All of this invites delay and interrupts the time-efficient flow of information. Ask for guidance and instruction from your department's IT manager or from your computer expert. Formulate a department-wide policy concerning the macro virus warnings. Learn what to do so as not to waste time when the warning next occurs.

Using Business Technology

There is a lot of technology at your disposal, which, when applied and used properly, will increase your productivity and save time. Unfortunately, we live in a world of constant upgrades in which we are told that our software and hardware need to be replaced. This transience keeps people in a state of constant learning, instead of allowing practical mastery.

It is certainly worthwhile to keep pace with the improvements in business technology, such as upgrading your computer, cell phone and software every couple of years, but you will only become efficient once you become proficient.

Take the Time to Master Your Tools

Whether you prefer to learn by experimenting, reading, or hiring a software coach, learn how to use some of the advanced features of your software. Most people never get past the first 10 percent of what a software application can do, which is a shame since many timesaving techniques can be realized with just a little more knowledge. If you hire a personal software coach, discuss what you want the software to do for you. Let your coach describe the techniques you need to learn. If you prefer to learn on your own or with a book, read the overview, find out what the software can do, then target those areas.

Don't strive to learn all the features at once, and don't bother to learn everything the software can do, but instead aim to master a few of the advanced features to the point at which they become automatic, meaning that they don't require a disruption of your thought processes in order to enact them.

Dishwasher Talk

Have you ever done the dishes or unloaded a dishwasher while talking on the phone? This is an example of two reasonably complicated manual skills being performed simultaneously. You are probably an expert at washing dishes or unloading a dishwasher because you've done it so many times. Little conscious effort is required, thus freeing you up to perform a second task: talking on the phone.

It is that level of expertise that you must strive for in mastering the key elements of your software. The ability to work automatically will be a major timesaver.

The difference between an expert and a non-expert is whether a particular skill can be performed without having to pull it into conscious memory. An expert is able to perform a task with seeming effortlessness.

Determine the skills you need, even if you don't know their correct terms. Do you need to know how to create a mail-merge, or add page numbers to a document, or create a 3-D graph or slide-show presentation, or update your virus-scanning software? If you need to do these things, then learn them completely. If not, then don't bother with them at all.

Learn About New Technologies

Many new tools become available each year in the areas of computing, scanning, communication, and information processing. Keep an ear to the ground to learn if any of these new tools would work for you. Some of them may save you time once you become comfortable with them.

Get a Technician to Set Up the Software and Hardware

Often, getting an expert to do the setup is a better use of your time than trying to configure it yourself. Whether you work from home or in an office, get to know your technicians. Make sure they're available to come and see you again if and when problems arise.

Plan for Problems and Have a Backup in Place

Your technology, as good as it is, will have problems on occasion. Make sure your contingency plans are in place. These should include having backup copies of your files on disk and on paper, the phone number of an on-call technician, and an alternate machine or resource upon which you can work.

Practice

It's the two-pound bucket once again. The time spent practicing techniques with your software will yield greater productivity for the rest of the time it is in use.

Use Virus-Scanning Software

Viruses are computer programs designed to do something you don't want them to. Some of these viruses are merely annoying, while others can be quite destructive. In this age of e-mail attachments, we must take care to ensure that the documents we send out are virus-free. This is considered the responsibility of the individual. Understanding how virus-scanning software works and how to keep it up-to-date is of great importance. People will wisely refuse to work with virus-infected data, which invites delay, as alternate copies have to be sent as replacements. It is far better from a time management and business relations point of view to make sure the files are safe before they leave.

To keep your virus-scanning software up-to-date, make sure to activate the software's "update" feature the next time you are connected to the Internet. This will send a message from your software to the manufacturer's Web site, asking for any update files. The software will install the update and reconfigure itself without any extra effort from you.

Thus, virus-scanning software deals with two time management issues at once: first, it ensures that the files with which you work are virus-free, which is a preemptive strike against the delays caused by the discovery of a virus; and second, the "update" feature of the anti-virus software itself means maintenance and updating is automatic, and can be done by the computer while you focus on other tasks.

Diagnostic and Maintenance Software

It is crucial that you keep your computer in optimum health. Machines tend to crash at the most inopportune moments, causing delay, stress, and expense. Many of your computer's problems can be avoided simply by using software dedicated to its upkeep. There are numerous brands of maintenance software that will monitor key computer issues such as memory allocation, disk space, and the fragmentation of the drives (whether data is stored neatly or messily). These software applications fall under the "ounce of prevention" rule. A healthy computer will run better, longer, allowing you to make better use of it and of your time.

Backup Software

From the same "ounce of prevention" camp comes backup software. It is crucial to bear in mind that your computer is merely a conduit. The true value of the machine lies in the data that you push through it. If water, fire, or theft were to render your machine unusable, it can be replaced. However, the information stored on that machine — and the time invested in creating it — may be lost forever.

If you work in an office environment, take time to find out the company's backup and storage policy. Make sure to transfer your most important files onto the network drive, especially if you carry a laptop.

For your own computer, invest in a backup system. This can take the form of high-density disks, writable CDs, tape backup, or off-site Internet storage. The time management issue here is that it takes far less time to pump the contents of a backup file back onto the hard drive of a new PC than it does to recreate the data from scratch.

Finally, nothing replaces paper as the ultimate backup. Print and store your most sensitive and crucial documents somewhere safe. This includes your Active Agenda. In a worst-case scenario, you can scan or reenter the data from the paper copy.

Surge Protectors

Lightning storms and power surges can damage a computer's sensitive insides in a fraction of a second. Invest in a high-quality surge protector with a tolerance of no more than two nanoseconds. Make sure the protector bar has input jacks for your computer's modem line as well as the power cord.

Word-Processing Shortcuts

Word-processing software contains numerous shortcuts that help shave time off repetitive tasks. Here are some techniques that are worth investing the time to learn:

- **Electronic shorthand**: Allows you to type simple initials like "mc" and have them be replaced instantly with "Merry Christmas."
- **Styles**: Records the way a paragraph is formatted, allowing you to apply the same attributes to subsequent paragraphs or change them all at one stroke.
- **Find and Replace**: Seeks out all instances of a word, replacing it with another word. The Find command by itself is also a handy technique for "jumping" to a particular location within a document without having to search for it.

The Personal Digital Assistant (PDA)

The Personal Digital Assistant, or PDA, is a handheld, self-contained mini-computer of sorts that fits easily in your pocket. It has its own operating system and runs a number of proprietary software programs. Its external features consist primarily of a screen, a stylus for entering information, and in some cases, a mini-keyboard. It is far more than an electronic Rolodex.

The PDA should be viewed as the perfect successor and sidekick to your computer, the logical next step. It lets you store a surprising amount of data and offers a number of highly interactive processing and communications features.

Your PDA can function almost like a second brain, dedicated to keeping track of the small details, keeping notes, and keeping in touch as much as you want to. Using your PDA to its fullest extent will help keep everything you need to succeed at your fingertips and let nothing fall by the wayside.

Your Active Agenda

To start with the basics, your PDA can store your appointment and contact information neatly and intelligently. Following the principles of the Active Agenda and the 60-second workspace, it keeps names, addresses, and dates in a single, searchable place, which can synchronize back to your computer-based calendaring software on your return to the office. Keeping names and addresses in a single container reduces time spent searching for a misplaced business card. Rescheduling an appointment no longer involves erasing and crossing out. A change of an appointment's start time is a matter of entering in the new numbers.

Taking Notes

Text can be entered into a PDA via a mini-keyboard or directly, by writing on the screen. But most people never master this skill, since the idea of writing on a mini-keyboard seems intricate and difficult to learn. But consider the advantages: When you are in a meeting, or an interview, or doing research, the notes you take into your PDA can later be pulled into your computer, eliminating the need to retype. If you have to type something more than once, you are wasting precious time.

Furthermore, by centralizing your notes on your PDA, you start to organize and control your world. You are building your 60-second workspace. You'll know where everything is. No more sticky notes stuck to walls and monitors, no more slips of paper stuffed into books, wallets, and briefcases. When you can find what you're looking for in less than 60 seconds, you start to pull ahead of the pack.

The PDA helps you note your ideas as they arrive. How many times have you had a thought or idea only to lose it again by a distraction? It is thought that every year, normal people such as ourselves each come up with ideas that could make millions of dollars if put into action. Do you really want to lose that next good idea? Learning how to write directly into your PDA requires practice. But like using computers, the Internet, or many other things in life, this practice will pay off. Get into the habit of jotting things down as soon as you think of them. With discipline, your PDA will act as a second brain, stopping things from slipping "through the cracks."

Connect, Copy, Paste

PDAs are designed to communicate with your computer, and the resulting conversations benefit you. For example, notes and memos entered into a PDA can be copied and pasted into word-processing documents. This means you can work on a report even when you're not near a computer. By copying relevant sections of a report into your PDA, you can edit, add to, and perfect the piece, and when you've finished, synchronize and copy the changed paragraphs back into the report. This is a great use of those spare minutes you might have while commuting, while waiting in an airport lounge, or before a meeting. If you find an interesting story on a Web page, and haven't the time to read it now, why not read it in the elevator? Select the text on the Web page, copy it, paste it into the PDA software, and then synchronize. Use the power of Copy and Paste to move information into and out of your PDA, making it a truly useful extension of your personal computer and an efficient time management tool.

E-mail

Use your PDA to connect to the Internet, to receive e-mail, to send or receive product or sales information, or even to surf the Web. Many on-line companies have created pages designed specifically for reading on a PDA screen, but all standard Web pages can be viewed on PDAs that are properly equipped. You can connect a PDA to the Internet either by way of a modem or antenna. You already know the Internet to be a central pillar in all aspects of business. Make sure you connect your PDA to the Net to get the information you need when you need it.

PDA technology will change and improve constantly. What is most important here, though, is to recognize it as a time management tool.

What should you consider, then, when choosing or starting to work with a PDA?

- **Writing:** Take the time to learn how to enter data into your PDA. Practice, and continue practicing until you can write at a satisfactory speed. Your ability to keep every scrap of information at your fingertips by entering it effortlessly into the PDA while you're on the road will keep you ahead of those people who can't write into a PDA very well, or those who don't use one at all.

- **Compatibility:** Make sure the PDA will work with your company's current setup. Is there a preferred brand that the company uses? Is it physically possible to connect the PDA to your computer at the office, or do network or other technical problems stand in the way? You will want to make sure the port that the PDA uses to communicate with the PC isn't being used by something else. Determine what your company uses as e-mail and spreadsheet software. Learn how the company connects to the Internet and the mail servers. How easy will it be to establish connections to deliver e-mail to the PDA? Will you be able to synchronize? Is there staff on hand to help? Certain calendaring software applications require third-party software to enable the synchronization of dates between a PDA and a computer. What does your company currently use for calendaring? The software may already be in place.

- **Confidentiality:** If you do plan to synchronize and carry data out onto your PDA, there is a risk that you may be compromising corporate security. As documents that are normally safely stored on a network are being carried out on a PDA, your company may have some security issues that are best dealt with in advance.

- **Home base:** Usually, a PDA prefers to synchronize to only one computer. Therefore, if you travel between a home office and a work office, you may want to decide which one is going to be the home base for the PDA. Even if the PDA is capable of synchronizing to two PCs, it is always safer to stick with one.

- **Back up!** As powerful as a PDA is, it is still a basic machine powered by batteries. Shock, cold, heat, static, and vibration may damage its memory and eliminate all the information inside. Make sure you have backup copies of all your data. If you synchronize to a computer, then your data will be duplicated on the computer itself. If you use the PDA by itself, you may want to consider sending a copy of your address book, calendar, and other important information to yourself via e-mail.

- **Spare batteries:** If your PDA runs on regular batteries rather than rechargeable ones, always carry a spare set with you. And read the instructions on how to change the batteries without affecting the memory.

There are many brands of PDA available, and they each have different features. Not all of them will offer the tools and features mentioned above. Some may offer different ones, and some may offer more. Take care before buying to make sure the PDA you choose is the one that will truly work for you.

The Personal Information Manager (PIM)

Personal Information Manager (PIM) refers to software that keeps track of your calendar, your contacts, and your tasks. A well-designed and well-used PIM should act as the hub of your operations. It should be the first thing you see as you start your I-Beam Review in the morning, and the last thing you see as you finish your second I-Beam Review in the evening.

Your PIM software should do the following:

- keep track of your appointments
- keep a searchable list of your contacts
- contain your To-Do list and Active Agenda
- ensure that uncompleted To-Do's are rolled over to the next day
- generate a minute-by-minute history of your time
- generate an event-by-event history of your clients, projects, and tasks
- remind you of recurring activities, including birthdays and anniversaries
- issue warnings and alarms for upcoming or conflicting appointments
- count down toward deadlines
- prompt you to schedule follow-ups and follow-throughs
- integrate with your word-processing software to create personalized documents
- print out calendar and contact information
- provide for easy rescheduling

- integrate and synchronize with PDAs
- create a backup of itself or remind you to do so regularly

You may already have a PIM on your computer. Perhaps you are already using it to schedule your appointments and to keep track of people and phone numbers. Here's your chance to fully exploit the technology.

Making full use of a PIM neither demands nor creates an obsession with record-keeping, but when you let a PIM keep track of day-to-day and repetitive events, as well as those things that would otherwise slip away unseen, you liberate yourself, allowing your mind to focus on more productive tasks such as strategizing, prioritizing, and creating.

The Precedent Checklist

Consider, for example, the principle of the precedent checklist. Think of all the activities that go into an event such as a meeting with a new potential client. You may need to research the client's company on the Internet, prepare a promotional package, and customize it with the client's name. You may need to set travel plans to arrive at the client's office in Cool Time. There should be at least one confirmation call and possibly a thank-you call scheduled for a few days later. This is a long list, possibly one that you will use again and again.

You can use your PIM to schedule all of these activities the moment that a new meeting comes up. Does that seem like a lot of work? Here's a way to make it less so. Choose a date way off in the future, such as January 1st, ten years from now. Create all the appointments and activities that go into a meeting, and schedule them in that week. It doesn't matter if in reality these activities don't actually happen in the same week; the point is to "corral" all of them in one "meeting sequence." Then, when a real meeting comes, you can copy and paste the corralled activities into the real dates corresponding to the real meeting. Doing this might take you all of 60 seconds, but in return, you arrive at your meeting fully and completely prepared.

Hyperlinks

PIMs are usually Internet-enabled. When you enter a person's e-mail or Web-page address into the appropriate field in the Contacts section, that entry will, when clicked, create a pre-addressed e-mail message or take you to the Web page, respectively. This is where the Contacts section of a PIM outshines a traditional Rolodex or paper-based address book, by providing instant connectivity to your contacts and resources through hyperlinks.

Documents

Most PIMs allow you to create a letter, invoice, memo, envelope, or other personalized document by way of a data merge with your word-processing application. Creating the templates for such data merges is a straightforward task that pays back in the savings of many minutes per day. And if you tend to write the same letters over and over again, such as confirmations, sales letters, or even invoices and quotations, creating a collection of merge templates with the standard text already written and with spaces for personalization such as salutations will save you time and also create consistency. Each PIM has a different command through which to create merged documents, but this is a technique that is worth mastering.

Attachments

Does your PIM allow you to electronically attach documents to individual contact entries? Many do, and if yours does, it is worth taking the time to learn how to use this key strategic feature. By attaching a saved, electronic version of a document to the contacts to whom the letter was originally sent, you will be able to create a logical knowledge thread in which all the documents related to a particular person are accessible through a single hyperlink. When files are attached to contacts, you are working in Cool Time by being able to immediately find all the relevant information on a particular client or project.

Timers

There are many times when keeping track of the time spent on a phone call or a project is important. If you bill your client or employer by the hour; if your project has a maximum number of hours to be spent; if you are forced to stop and start on a particular task throughout the day; or if you spend a lot of time with your clients on the phone, it can be very difficult to keep track of the time spent.

The one thing better than time spent is time paid for. Using a timer to time your billable activities will allow you to potentially regain thousands of dollars over a year — dollars billed to the client that otherwise would have been absorbed as day-to-day expenses. Even if you work on a salary, keeping track of where your time goes helps you to plan for more effective time management during your I-Beam Review and Bird's-Eye View periods.

Take a moment to learn where the timer is on your PIM. Practice using it until you are able to activate it automatically as you answer the phone or as you start upon a new task. If your

PIM does not have a timer, consider using a physical timer or stopwatch.

PDA Connection

By setting up your PIM to talk to your PDA, you have the best of both worlds. Your PDA takes your calendar, contacts, and tasks with you on the road. While you're out on the road, any new information you enter into your PDA will be delivered to your PIM when you next synchronize.

Project Management Software

Many of the time management principles put forth in this book are based on project management. Project management is about planning, communication, and control. Projects change over time, and a project plan must therefore be flexible, yet it must also leave nothing to chance. Though a PIM or even a paper-based calendar may suffice for your day-to-day activities, the use of project management software for your overall projects, both professional and personal, makes their management and planning much easier.

The benefit of using project management software is that your planned activity grows in front of you, even as you think it through for the first time. It is an excellent tool when planning projects that include more than one person or consist of more than a few tasks. It is also extremely useful for back-planning, in which you start at the deadline date and work backwards, filling in all the tasks, and arriving at the critical path start date. The software can help not only projects with a fixed end date, but can also serve as a key tool in dealing with procrastination. In addition, project management software keeps track of weekends, holidays, and other constraints while you plan.

Project management software should be, and is, easy to use. It generally consists of a screen layout in which each task and subtask can be depicted by horizontal bars, representing the task over time, in what is called a Gantt chart. These can easily be moved, rescheduled, and linked, as is so necessary when maintaining and controlling a project of any size. It comes as a surprise to many just how quickly a simple task reveals itself to be a collection of subtasks. This is good, as it sets a clear, realistic path toward the attainment of a goal.

In addition to being easy to use, project management software should also have the capacity to generate reports, to communicate information and progress, and to offer statistics about the project.

Voice Recognition Software

Voice recognition software, which transcribes dictated text to word-processing software, is a crucial time management tool on two fronts. First, it is a superb replacement for typing. If your keyboarding skills are less than fluid, much time can be wasted as your fingers struggle to keep up with your thoughts. Voice recognition software receives and processes text at the speed of standard speech, allowing a document to be created and edited much more quickly and efficiently.

Voice recognition offers a second time management advantage through its potential for sheer productivity. By removing the need for the manual effort of pounding the keyboard, your body and mind are free to adopt a much more relaxed posture. You could look up at the ceiling, stare through the window, or even ride an exercise bike. Your arms and shoulders are no longer locked in "keyboard position." Your spine and muscles are free to move and stretch. Your conscious and subconscious minds are released from over-concentration, and your eyes are no longer required to stare incessantly at the screen. Fatigue, muscle stiffness, and the risk of longer-term repetitive stress injuries are reduced — which, in combination with the creative freedom that voice recognition allows, makes it an essential tool for even the swiftest of typists.

Voice recognition does require an initial investment of an hour or so to build a preliminary voice file, in which the computer gets used to the particular timbre and peculiarities of your speech. But this initial investment, like so many other time management techniques, pays off quickly through its productivity and efficiency. In this case, the software continues to learn, taking note of your speech patterns and building a more personalized, accurate profile as you work. Basically, the more you use it, the better it becomes, and in turn, the better you become.

In addition to the traditional approach of simply dictating a singular document through voice recognition software, consider these additional time management techniques:

- **Multiple e-mails:** Your e-mail software may not have a voice recognition component built in, but that shouldn't stop you from taking full advantage of voice recognition. Simply dictate all of your e-mails as one single voice recognition document, separating each unique letter by two or three paragraph lines. Once you have finished dictating the text for all of your letters, select the paragraphs specific to letter one, and cut and paste them into the body area of e-mail one. Then select the paragraphs specific to letter two, and cut and paste them into the body area of e-mail two, and so on. In short, dictate all of your prose into one long "working document," and then distribute accordingly.

- **Multiple documents.** If you find yourself working on two or more documents simultaneously, there is no need to have to switch back and forth between them if your mind and body are currently in dictation mode. If you're in the middle of dictating the text for document one and an idea for document two jumps into your head, simply start a new paragraph within the same document, with the opening words "For document two." Dictate the appropriate text, then return, in the next paragraph, to the work of document one. At the end of your voice recognition session, cut and paste the paragraphs for document two into their proper document. Just as with the e-mail example above, dictate all of your prose into one long "working document," and then distribute accordingly.

- **Free flow of consciousness:** There will be times when the best ideas come not in a linear fashion, but through a flow-of-consciousness approach. Voice recognition excels at this, since it frees you even further from the constraints of grammar, recording your thoughts and ideas as they tumble forward. If you are in the beginning stages of a creative process, activate your voice recognition software, close your eyes, and let the thoughts flow free. Once the dictation session is over and the document is saved, your transcribed thoughts will be very easy to clean up and rearrange.

- **PDA and PIM entries:** If you use a PDA as a time management and personal organization tool, there is great practicality in using voice recognition software to dictate notes to yourself, which can then be synchronized to your PDA for use on the road. Similarly, if you use PIM software as your personal calendar or address book, quick notes to yourself dictated into the middle of a formal report can be cut and pasted very quickly and easily — even though there may not be direct voice recognition compatibility. This fulfils the important time management principle of recording everything. It is wiser to nail down stray thoughts right away than to lose them forever.

Master the Commands

In addition to transcribing your words, voice recognition software also enables you to move the text around to create a new paragraph, or to select and change a word or sentence. Take the time to learn these navigational commands. Commit them to memory. The goal is to be able to dictate commands to the cursor faster by voice than you could do with the mouse or keyboard. Once you can do this, and you can talk to your computer as easily as talking on the phone, you will be a voice recognition expert.

Train It

Voice recognition software has to listen to your voice and figure out what you are saying. This process is ongoing. The more you use the software, the better it will get. Take the time to train it at the outset, and then master the art of correcting words that it gets wrong in such a way as to make sure it gets them right the next time. By mastering these training commands, you will develop a smooth, fast relationship with this valuable tool.

Focus on clear speech. Practice clear enunciation. The clearer your words are, the better the software will perform.

Text-to-Speech Software

Text-to-speech software reads back printed text. Many people have trouble proofreading their own work, and this is understandable. It is very difficult to spot the errors in something you have just created. Text-to-speech software allows more diligence in the creative process, since it reads out loud what it sees on the screen, enabling you to hear your mistakes and correct them on the fly. Text-to-speech software also allows for a period of reflection while you hear your written work read back to you.

People don't always see the value in this type of technology. But business success still revolves around the written word. Documents, reports, e-mail, and Web pages distribute and present the written word faster than ever before. There is enormous pressure to create and release documents quickly, sometimes before they can be thoroughly proofed and checked. However, any temporary satisfaction felt from getting a document off your desk is quickly extinguished when errors are revealed and it is sent back for revision.

This is where the time management component of text-to-speech technology kicks in. It allows you to take a Bird's-Eye View of your work, to be diligent and accurate, and to make your work complete and excellent.

Also, as is the case with voice recognition software, there are physical benefits to using text-to-speech software. Every time you can break away from the standard upright position of sitting at a keyboard, even just to look out the window or to get up and walk around, you help to reduce eye and neck strain and lower back pain. You help maintain good circulation and you allow your body and mind to relax while still maintaining productivity.

13

Getting Started

There remains one more time management principle to discuss, and that is how to get started. As with many great endeavors, the first step may be daunting and difficult to integrate. Or, it may seem insignificant in the face of the major changes to come. Either way, you face a challenge in modifying the momentum of your life and of the lives of those around you. Change requires dedication, but it must also be natural. There will be certain things that just will not "go" with your personality, your job, or your priorities. But everything must have a beginning. If you can resolve to initiate a new plan of action, to commit to making the changes over a period of a month without falling back, and to review your actions and goals on a regular basis, you will be able to fuel your spirit with the dedication and motivation needed for success.

Committing to the Process

Make a firm commitment in your mind that you will embark on these time management techniques. Write this commitment down on paper where you and your family can see it. Start to develop the habits and implement the techniques described in this book, taking care to weave them into the tapestry of your own life, with its unique priorities, goals, and rules.

Committing to a Clean-Up

You may need a physical clean-up, involving an afternoon one Sunday putting files away, creating a computerized docket ledger, and building your 60-second workspace. If so,

- **Be ruthless.** Focus on the end result, which is your smoothly running, functioning office.
- **Stow or throw.** As you clean up, process every piece of paper, every file, and every other item in your workspace. Put each away in an appropriate place or throw it away.
- **Don't reminisce.** Avoid distractions while cleaning up just as you would during your Keystone Period or while doing research on the Internet. Don't get caught up in documents or photographs that break the momentum. If they're that important, put them in a "reminiscence file" for reviewing during your non-work period.
- **Create your 60-second workspace.** Start by creating and coordinating your files with your file index. Remember that everything that takes your attention, from office projects to family and personal files, should be assigned a docket number, a file, and if necessary, a computer disk.
- **Remove all sticky notes.** Enter messages and phone

number information into your contact management software or your day timer. Keep it central and keep it tidy.

In addition to the physical clean-up, commit to a mental clean-up. Tell yourself that this is the start of a new system, a system that will work, a system that will give you more time to do the things you truly want to do.

- **Make a list of all time-wasters.** Think of the activities that swallow your time. From coffee breaks to traffic jams to meetings, assess each one as to its relevance and importance. Ask yourself whether you can schedule, remove, or otherwise deal with it according to your time management principles.
- **Analyze current corporate culture.** How is your office running currently? What improvements could you gradually introduce to help other people become more time-effective?
- **Factor in the changes pragmatically.** Though you may wish to implement every single time management technique immediately, sometimes a wholesale change of office lifestyle may prove too difficult for you and your colleagues to take. Instead, set up a plan to factor in key time management techniques gradually, slowly influencing the timing of meetings, introducing the Keystone Period perhaps one day a week at the start, and "grandfathering" existing projects and priorities so as not to jeopardize current operations. Remember, your time management skills are designed to last a long time, and your success in implementing them may rely on easing them into your life.
- **Be sure to maintain a good "credit rating" with your peers.** Your colleagues, superiors, and staff will all need to understand and believe in your new time management

activities. Some may be interested in working alongside you, while others may reject the principles outright. Make sure to communicate the principles to them so that all of your colleagues become familiar with the benefits of a carefully managed day, but also be sensitive to their particular doubts and deadlines. Those who gradually accept the techniques of time management may be willing to try them for themselves, which will help spread the techniques across the office, and in turn magnify their positive effects. Other colleagues will not accept the principles or may simply not be able to use them, and these people must therefore be dealt with as constraints to your own plans.

- **Use a buddy system.** Consider starting out on the road to time management success with a colleague — perhaps someone with whom you work, or perhaps someone in a completely different business or office. Your mutual support and awareness will help maintain your time management principles and techniques, especially during times of weakness. Use each other's experiences for mutual support.

- **Schedule review periods.** Regular reviews of your achievements and conflicts with the time management regime are crucial. Schedule a review period for one month, three months, six months, and a year after your kickoff date. Take a Bird's-Eye View of your time management process, refocus your energies, and control the project itself.

In Conclusion:
The Benchmark Bookmark

Time management is about control — control over your own destiny, from the next few minutes to the rest of your life. It's a very personal system that can and should be maintained only by you. It requires diligence, tact, and communication skills for its several parts to interact neatly with the people, priorities, and activities of your world.

The techniques and principles mentioned in this book are merely suggestions. If they prove to be counterproductive or a hindrance, don't use them. Many of them will take a little time to get right. Choose those that fit your lifestyle and work at them.

Most people "fall off the wagon" when starting a new regime because they don't give themselves enough time before giving up. For a new system to become a habit, you must work at it for at least 20 days. So, in parting, I have an assignment for you:

Identify your most pressing time management problems, and write them down, now, while the Cool Time principles are still fresh in your mind. Next to each one, write down what you plan to do to change and improve it. Then write down *why* you wish to make these changes. Identify and target the underlying motivation(s) that will help keep you on the straight and narrow path to time management success. You could be motivated by anything from spending more time with your family or being able to enjoy your Sunday without getting uptight over the approaching Monday, to reducing stress at work or having more control over meetings or projects.

When your resolve starts to falter, reread your list. Reconnect with why these changes are important to you. Carry the list with you as your benchmark of success. Use it as a bookmark inside the next book you read, and the one after that, and the one after that. Just as you learned to do with the Active Agenda principle in Chapter 5, make your plans real by getting them down on paper

Of all the reasons for employing time management, I get the most satisfaction from knowing that I have control over my own destiny. Although there are always outside influences to contend with, the power I do have fuels my motivation and makes every day enjoyable.

Please feel free to contact me at any time to ask questions, offer comments or suggestions, or share your experiences with time management. You can reach me directly at **prentice@bristall.com**, and you can visit the Cool Time Web site at **www.cool-time.com**.

Good luck, and keep hold of that bucket!

Index